FATHERL

IDENTITIES OF A CUBAN AMERICAN

BY

CHARLES LOPEZ BRUNS

While every precaution has been taken in the preparation of this book, the publisher assumes no responsibility for errors or omissions, or for damages resulting from the use of the information contained herein.

FATHERLANDS: IDENTITIES OF A CUBAN AMERICAN

First edition: October 2021

ISBN: 978-1-7377980-1-9 (digital)

ISBN: 978-1-7377980-0-2 (paperback)

Written by Charles Lopez Bruns

Published by Charles Anthony Communication

Media and permissions: CharlesAnthonyComm@gmail.com

Table of Contents (print edition)

This book is dedicated to Cuban Americans and all the children of immigrants whose families have come to the United States – and will continue doing so—for a better life.

It is also dedicated to everyone from lands across our world who have never felt unconditional love from a father.

Author's Note

This book is a memoir. It reflects my present recollections of experiences that took place over the course of my lifetime. Some events have been compressed, and some dialogue has been recreated. Some names have been changed for privacy protection. When necessary, events have been verified by family and friends and information has been confirmed by research and other documentation.

Identity

1.   a. the distinguishing character or personality of an individual: individuality
           b. the relation established by psychological identification
2. the condition of being the same with something described or asserted * establish the identity of stolen goods
3.   a. sameness of essential or generic character in different instances
           b. sameness in all that constitutes the objective reality of a thing: oneness
4. an equation that is satisfied for all values of the symbols
5. identity element

—from Merriam-Webster dictionary app

"Having an identity can enable people to have a sense of belonging which can potentially lead to better feelings of well-being and confidence."

—from   https://www.childrenssociety.org.uk/mental-health-advice-for-children-and-young-people/identity

Prelude: Fatherlands: Identities of a Cuban American

As the sun was setting one early evening in mid-April 1961, a four-year-old boy looked out the window of the Havana, Cuba, home his *tía abuela* (Spanish for grand aunt) and *tío abuelo* (grand uncle) shared with him. He saw dozens of young men, some of them throwing on their shirts while clutching a few belongings, frantically running out onto the street, and jumping into the backs of slow-moving trucks.

"*¡Vamos a luchar contra los Americanos!*" ("Let's go fight the Americans!") the little boy heard the young men yell. Some of them were angry, others simply excited. The boy was stunned by the commotion as neighbors spilled onto the street, watching the trucks slowly fill with loud young men. He turned to his *tía abuela* and *tío abuelo* and said, "*Pero yo soy Americano.*" ("But I'm an American.")

That was the start of the boy's twisting, turning journey with his identity. That boy was me.

In the following pages, I will share with you how Charles Anthony Lopez became Charles Anthony Bruns. You will read how a Cuban American boy's identity evolved as he became an American man. Along the way, you will read what it was like for me to be a New York kid and New Jersey guy during the second half of the 20th century, how I struggled with the father figures who bestowed their names on me, the impact my identity had on my own family and career and who I have become today.

We are defined by who we are and who we are not. Come along for the ride and perhaps you will learn more about not only me, but possibly yourself and millions of others around our diverse world whose identities are being transformed by immigration, separation, condemnation, assimilation, cultural changes or, ultimately, their own self-realization.

El Niño in Cuba

PART 1: "Charlito Lopez"
Chapter 1. El Niño: An American in Revolutionary Cuba

I was born in New York City in 1956 and spent my pre-school years divided between the West Side of Manhattan and Cuba. I have no memories of my life in New York before I was six years old. But many years later, my mother told me that when I was four years old, she walked with me a few blocks from our public housing project to a block with old tenements which were getting ready to be razed. On 68th Street between Amsterdam and West End avenues we watched some of the filming of the *West Side Sto*ry movie that would be released to much acclaim in 1961. I don't remember that, but thankfully my mother saved dozens of pictures she took of my older brother and me. In these photos, we look just like what any other young family in our Amsterdam Houses neighborhood, typically referred to as "the projects," must have looked like, celebrating birthdays and other events in our two-bedroom apartment, and having fun in the playgrounds.

My parents, Elena and Humberto, were both born in Cuba to white parents of Spanish descent. My mother grew up in the Havana area as an only child. She was just four years old when her *padre* (father), Alberto, died from appendicitis in 1940. While being raised by her late father's family, my mother completed her education around 1953. Within a few months, she left Cuba for New York City and reunited with her *madre* (mother), Belen. My widowed *abuela* (grandmother) had moved out of her in-laws' home and emigrated to New York City in 1947, when my mother was eleven years old.

My father, who was two years older than my mother, grew up in Havana as the oldest of three children. His mother, Abuela Nina, was a well-kept woman and talented opera singer who focused more on her family than a career. His father, my *abuelo* (grandfather), worked at a bank as an accountant. Abuelo Elpidio was also a musician, I was told many years later. My grandparents' housekeeper helped raise my father and their two other children. Abuela Nina was the disciplinarian in the family while Abuelo Elpidio was relatively gentle.

My parents began dating in Havana before my mother turned seventeen, when she left for New York City. My father followed my mother shortly afterward and they married in New York during the spring of 1954.

Just as they gave their first-born son, my brother, an American first name ("Louis") and middle name ("Albert") in 1955, my parents decided to name me "Charles," not "Carlos" a year later. For my middle name, they chose "Anthony" instead of "Antonio." They were proud of starting an American family in their new country. At the time, judging by the names of some neighbors and classmates a few years later, it was common for Hispanics in New York City to bestow Spanish names on their U.S.-born children, but a few chose anglicized names instead. Nearly all Hispanics and other U.S. immigrants during the 1950s wanted their children to quickly assimilate into American culture, regardless of whether their first name was English or not. My parents decided to begin the process with the identities of their children.

Things are not always what they seem, I've learned time and time again. By all accounts, my parents did not have a happy marriage by the time I learned to walk, if ever. On a couple of occasions while they were married, my mother went to Cuba without my father for extended periods. The first time was in late autumn 1955, when my brother Lou was less than a year old and my mother was pregnant with me. The second was in December 1957, when I was just a year old.

My first memories are of being in Cuba with Lou when we returned in the winter of 1960 for a few months. By that time, Fidel Castro had been in power for over a year and some of the island's inhabitants were fleeing in fear of their lives. Relations had not yet soured much between Cuba and the United States, but some Cubans and Americans felt that perhaps the charismatic Cuban leader was not all that he appeared to be. Political opponents were being persecuted and there were signs that Castro's Cold War sympathies were with the Soviet Union rather than the U.S. Still, many Cubans, both on the island and in the U.S., were hopeful that the fall of Dictator Fulgencio Batista would usher in better times in Cuba. These included Cubans who, for economic opportunities, had settled in the West Side of Manhattan and other parts of New York City.

My maternal grandmother, Abuela Belen, was among the Cubans who began living in the Upper West Side of Manhattan twelve years before the Revolution triggered a bigger wave of Cuban migration to the U.S. Up until the 1940s, most Cubans who emigrated to the United States settled in Florida. Tampa was a popular destination for many.

Widowed for seven years at that point, Abuela Belen began working as a seamstress in Manhattan's Garment District when she arrived in New York City in 1947. Within four years, Belen married Juan, a Chilean American U.S. Merchant Marine she met in New York. Just as Belen was a very attractive and fashionable woman well into her thirties—all her life, actually—her new husband was a very suave and style-conscious man. (But later in life, I simply remembered him as a drunk who owned the first color TV I ever saw.) They had a son, my Uncle John, my mother's half-brother, who would become one of the most important male figures in my life.

I guess Abuela Belen, who proved to be the sweetest and most inspirational woman in my life, was very busy working and raising her son while her husband was on a ship somewhere around the world. She neglected to take care of the paperwork needed to legally remain in the U.S. An immigration official hauled her and my very young Uncle John away to Ellis Island, where they were confined for one night before getting placed on a plane back to Cuba. While there, Belen did what was required to be allowed back into the U.S. with John, who was born in 1951 in New York and, therefore, an American citizen.

My family was among those Cuban Americans who liked Castro at first. We turned out to cheer for him and enthusiastically wave Cuban flags when he came to New York City in April 1959, just a few months after seizing power in Cuba. But by the time Castro returned to New York in September 1960, he had begun nationalizing U.S. businesses in Cuba and ruffling the feathers of American government officials, who responded by implementing a partial economic embargo on Cuba that October.

My parents divorced by late 1960, and my father left my mother alone to raise my brother and me in our apartment in Amsterdam Houses. The development, built in 1948 and at the time still among the newest in that part of the West Side, consisted of thirteen red brick buildings with over 1,000 units on nine acres between West 61st and 64th streets and Amsterdam and West End avenues. It had two playgrounds, was within two blocks of two elementary schools and two high schools and was only three blocks west of Central Park.

The neighborhood was a good location for a divorcee to raise two young boys, but my mother Elena had no job, few marketable skills, no advanced education and, unlike my father, little grasp of the English language. She did listen to Spanish-language radio and read Spanish-language newspapers, which undoubtedly covered with some degree of accuracy the rising tension between Cuba and the U.S. as 1960 turned to 1961.

Against this backdrop, my mother arranged for me to go to Cuba for a few months in early 1961, even though diplomatic relations between the two countries were officially severed that January 3. My mother needed to find work, but she realized she wouldn't be able to afford to pay a babysitter to watch me as well as my brother when he got home from kindergarten if she was to clear enough money to cover her bills. She figured someone could watch Lou for a few hours each day, but wanted me to be watched all day at no charge for a few months. Abuela Belen was working full-time and had her hands full trying to raise Uncle John while his father was away most of the time, so she couldn't help. Tía Abuela Paki, who was Belen's older sister, and her husband, Tío Abuelo Ramon, living in the Jaimanitas neighborhood of Havana, agreed to take me in. Paki looked and acted much like Belen, which was comforting to me. I remember Ramon as a big man with sunglasses, wearing a guayabera shirt and smoking a cigar who never raised his voice.

Shortly after I began living in Cuba with Tía Abuela Paki and Tío Abuelo Ramon in the winter of 1961, as my fifth birthday approached, the ill-fated Bay of Pigs invasion occurred. I looked out the window of their home to see the young men jumping on trucks to fight the Americans. Relations between Cuba and the U.S. got even worse, which prevented me from returning to New York after a few months as my mother had hoped. So, Paki and Ramon took care of me for over eighteen months, during which time I turned six.

In the fall of 1961, I was enrolled in kindergarten, along with all the other children in my Havana neighborhood. I lasted all of three days. The Communist government's brainwashing of Cuban youth had begun. As the red, white, and blue Cuban flag hung in our classroom, a teacher told my classmates and me in no uncertain terms that Castro and his Revolution would provide for us. I came home after school one day and told Tía Abuela Paki and Tío Abuelo Ramon that I did not need to go back home to New York because Castro would take care of everything I needed right there in Cuba. I never went back to class, either because my family decided it was not a good idea for me to be exposed to the Communist ideology or because the school decided against continuing to educate an American citizen. The experience made me feel different from the other young boys in my Jaimanitas neighborhood, all of whom went to school during the day and must have considered me an outcast or worse at the time. In any case, I still like to say I'm a kindergarten dropout who went on to get a master's degree.

Nearly all of my days during this extended stay in Cuba were spent around Tía Abuela Paki and Tío Abuelo Ramon's home in a row of attached one-story apartment units right on the shore of the Caribbean Sea. It was quite picturesque, as you can imagine. The stairs behind their apartment led down to a common concrete landing, from where we could set foot in the sea. When the tide was low, we could wade part of the way out to the lighthouse about a half-mile from the shore. But when storms struck, the sea waters would actually cover the common concrete landing, rise over the back stairs, and enter our apartment. More than once, as I laid in bed, I watched the sea waters flow in and out of our home. It was frightening, but Paki and Ramon stayed calm. Little got ruined inside our homes because the floors were concrete and anything of value was elevated out of harm's way.

Most days I was in Cuba during 1961-62 seemed sunny and beautiful. But I missed my mother and brother and wondered when I would be back in New York with them. These thoughts must have weighed heavily on my mind because by some accounts I was an ill-tempered child. One day my aunt and her boyfriend came to visit me. Unlike her brothers, one of whom was my father, Tía Gloria and her parents, my paternal grandparents, had not yet emigrated to the U.S. She gave me a present when she saw me, and I responded to her kindness by smashing the toy on the curb right in front of her and her boyfriend, who eventually became my uncle. Tío Basilio (or "Basi") reminded me of this incident one evening fifty years later as we sat around his Hialeah, Florida home drinking one *cortadito* coffee after another with Gloria, who was his wife of over forty-five years by then. Basi reminded me of another time when I chased him with a stick when he and Gloria visited me while I was in Cuba. "*El niño*" ("the boy") has "*candela*," he said, which is Cuban-speak for a person on fire or a troublemaker. In hindsight, I must have been acting out my anger over missing my mother and brother.

A recurring memory of that time was riding my tricycle around the changing rooms and lockers located across the street from my home, which was right next to a bar and beach. Since Americans had stopped visiting Cuba by that time, the area was typically quiet except for day trippers from around Havana who needed a place to change into their bathing suits and back into street clothes. Tío Abuelo Ramon and his friends often played dominoes on a table by the changing rooms. I still remember the sounds of the ivory dominoes being shuffled between hands. I also recall the aroma of the espresso coffee Tía Abuela Paki would serve the men while they were playing. To this day, the sound of dominoes and the aroma of espresso are among my favorites. And I still enjoy the fragrance of Havana cigars like the ones Ramon and his friends, and many Cubans, would smoke.

One of my earliest memories of feeling different from my peers took place during that period as a kindergarten dropout in Havana. There was a store a few blocks from my home that had a display of flashlights for sale under a glass counter. A particular flashlight that was a little more expensive than the others caught my fancy. Somehow, I saved up enough coins after a while to buy it, and some of the bigger boys in the neighborhood took note of the little American with the new flashlight. At least one of these boys also took a fancy to the same flashlight. One day, I found myself surrounded by these bigger boys, each with their own, older flashlights, who decided to play a game that was a version of musical chairs. But instead of changing chairs we were trading flashlights around until one of the older boys stopped talking. At that moment, everyone got to keep the flashlight that was in their hands. My nice new flashlight, of course, wound up in the hands of the boy who decided when to stop talking. I had an old, worn-out flashlight in my hands. The boys walked away, laughing, and saying some derogatory things about Americans as I stood there, almost in tears.

Another memory from those days in Havana was the time I stepped on a nail in the empty lot next to the row of homes where I lived. The lot was full of debris, and I don't know why I was walking around barefoot in it except that I was a five-year-old boy who simply didn't know better. As soon as the long nail lodged itself in my heel, I fell down on all four limbs howling in pain. I crawled about fifty yards towards my home, the sound of my wailing eventually catching the attention of Tía Abuela Paki. She pulled the piece of wood containing the nail in my heel away from my foot, and I still remember the bloody hole left by the nail. A doctor arrived shortly to clean and bandage the wound, and I stayed in bed for a few days to let it heal. To this day, I don't like walking barefoot, not even on the clean floors of my own house. The only exception is walking on a beach. This is probably because I enjoyed walking barefoot on sand even as a little boy by my home in Cuba.

When the August day in 1962 finally arrived for me to return to New York, I was ushered into a small office building where an armed and bearded man stood guard. Although I was excited by the prospect of seeing my mother and brother again, I was sad to be leaving Tía Abuela Paki and Tío Abuelo Ramon. I had spent every day with them for the past twenty months but would never see them again. They decided to remain in their Jaimanitas seaside home and passed away within ten years, well before the U.S. allowed its residents to travel to the island.

When my plane landed in Miami, a couple I did not recognize greeted me at the airport. My mother told me afterward they were extended family members. The couple gave me the choice of going to their home that evening on a motorcycle (I did not have any luggage) and taking a plane to New York City the next morning, or immediately getting on another plane to New York. Frightened by the prospect of riding on the back of a motorcycle—but not scared of getting on another plane—I quickly chose to continue my journey home that evening.

I fell asleep on the flight home and was awakened by a young and pretty stewardess after every other passenger had gotten off the plane. My mother and brother were waiting for me at the New York airport, and we rode home in a taxicab late that night. I was excited to be re-united with them, but more than anything I was just tired after a long and emotional day. Lou never stopped talking to me that night and my mother never stopped smiling. It was her birthday—August 24—and her second son had finally returned home. I eventually made my way into the bedroom of our apartment that I would continue sharing with Lou for the next five years.

I fell asleep to the sound of his voice that evening. It was nice to be back home.

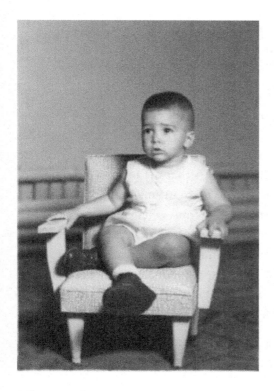

The Second Son at 1½ years

Chapter 2. The Second Son: Divorced Catholics

My mother and father divorced when I was four years old, shortly before my twenty-month stay in Cuba. I never got a definitive explanation on why they divorced, but my mother did tell me years later that she had evidence my father had girlfriends on the side. But I've also been told by my father's family members that my mother was "the only love of his life." My father did wind up marrying and divorcing three times, and there had been stretches of time when my mother was in Cuba with my brother and me while he had stayed behind in New York, a city full of attractive young women. Getting married at relatively young ages—my mother had been just seventeen and my father nineteen when they wed—and being immature and without counseling also might have contributed to their divorce.

By the time I was six and had returned from Cuba for the last time, my mother had no kind words to say about my father. But she did tell me a funny story about him that I've never forgotten. Apparently, sometimes my father would have enough money to buy a used car. Once, he got an old car that was in need of a paint job, so he got a can of paint and a brush and began painting the car by hand in front of our Amsterdam Avenue apartment building. According to my mother, a man in a car pulled up to my father and yelled, "You must be Cuban!"

After the divorce, it seems my father rarely paid the child support due monthly to my mother. She loathed the sight of him when he would come by every month or two to take my brother and me out for part of a day. Lou and I did not particularly look forward to these outings. They were rarely fun. Typically, we would accompany our father as he visited friends in the downtown Brooklyn, Brooklyn Heights, and Cobble Hill neighborhoods around his new home on Hoyt Avenue.

We would go from one apartment to another as our father talked and gambled with his friends.

One time my mother thought it would be a good idea for my brother and me to bring along a few boxes of the chocolate bars we needed to sell for our school's fundraiser. It turned out to be a bad idea. A very bad idea. As we visited our father's friends that afternoon, Lou and I were happy to be selling a lot of our candy bars, which were not cheap at fifty cents to a dollar apiece. We had sold all our candy by the time we accompanied our father to the last of the homes of his card-playing friends. The problem was that the cards were not kind to our father that afternoon. When he ran out of money, he started gambling the dollars Lou and I had earned selling candy to his friends.

"I'll start winning and give you back the candy money and more so you can buy some for yourselves," our father said after my brother and I reluctantly handed over our little fistfuls of dollar bills and coins to him. His friends looked at us and said nothing.

And he continued losing. He brought us back to our mother that evening with no money—and no candy—as my mother screamed at him for being so irresponsible.

Aside from playing cards, my father also liked to gamble at the racetrack. On more than one occasion, his idea of a nice family outing with his two sons was to go to Aqueduct Racetrack or another track to watch "*los caballos*" (the horses). I don't think I ever saw my father as excited as when his horse won. The more his horse paid, the more excited he was. To this day, whenever I visit a racetrack, I think of my father. And there's always a voice in my head that keeps saying, "*los caballos!*"

Sometimes my father would leave us with his second wife and her two daughters at their apartment while he went out for a few hours. This must have been very awkward for his new wife, an older Hispanic woman, but she was kind to my brother and me. Her daughters, who were only a few years older than us, just avoided talking to us.

At other times our father would bring us to the apartment of his brother, Tío Pete, in Brooklyn and disappear for a few hours. Pete was four years younger, taller, and thinner than Humberto. His heavyset wife, Tía Grace, was an especially nice woman who taught Lou and me how to play Monopoly and a couple of other games. Their son, my little cousin Petey, was always with us and the four of us would pass the time as best as we could. Grace had to be a patient and loving woman to be married for over a dozen years to Pete, who was a bit of a wild man. I remember once he came home with a full head of steam, bloodied after a fight, and rolled some newspaper around a metal pipe while muttering angrily to himself before quickly leaving in a huff to get revenge on his nemesis.

Like my father, Tío Pete wound up marrying three times during his short life.

When my father and mother divorced, Humberto left behind a number of things for me. He left me with his surname and, time would reveal, some of his physical traits. There is no question that my oval face and prominent chin, thick eyebrows, brown eyes, a nondescript nose, and a mouth that can open to a wide smile, topped by a full head of dark hair (in my younger years, anyway), resembles his. He was not a bad-looking guy—my mother must have thought he was handsome at some point—so I was okay with the resemblance. In pictures when my father and mother were married and starting our family, he had a robust build. Eventually, he became obese. At one point during my college years, I gained almost thirty pounds and looked exactly like he had at the same age. Fortunately for my health, I dropped the thirty pounds by the time I graduated and have kept them off.

Sometimes when my mother would get especially mad at me for something I did while growing up, she would tell me, "Oh, you remind me of your father!" I knew I had greatly angered and disappointed her when I heard those words. It made me feel terrible. But I knew it was also partly because of how I looked. Lou didn't look anything like our father and was never subjected to that comment from our mother.

My father lost a lot of weight late in his life. Before he turned fifty, after living in Miami for over ten years, he became quite ill. He left his job driving a truck for the Miami-Dade County Sanitation Department (now Department of Solid Waste Management), and returned to Brooklyn to be with his sister, Tía Gloria. She worked at a hospital in an administrative support function and tried to help him. My wife and I visited him at Gloria's home in Brooklyn in 1983. I was taken aback by how frail and old he looked; he seemed forty-nine years old going on seventy. But it was a pleasant visit. We talked like long lost friends rather than father and son. We spoke about family and friends we both knew and what we had been doing over the dozen or so years since we had last seen each other. He made a point to tell me he drove a garbage truck but did not pick up the trash. It was the only time my wife saw him. And the last time I did. He passed away four years later in Miami, where he returned to spend time with his brother, Tío Pete, his niece Anna and, eventually when she moved to southern Florida, his sister, Gloria. The cause of death at age fifty-three was an enlarged heart. It was a shame I rarely got to feel the good side of his "big" heart. But he did inadvertently teach me how *not* to be a father, a lesson I would learn again. The facial similarity he left me also continues to remind me who I am, the son of a Cuban man of Spanish descent who immigrated to the U.S.

Except for their shared ethnicity, my mother was the exact opposite of my father. Although I've been told my father did not drink more than an occasional beer, my mother didn't drink any alcohol whatsoever. As irresponsible as he was, my father didn't seem to have any problem find-ing work. He taught himself to speak good English, and he was handy enough by nature to figure out almost anything that needed to be done. But one thing he did not do was pay alimony or child support with any regularity after he and my mother divorced. My mother, on the other hand, struggled to learn English until she enrolled in a class with other Spanish-speaking adults. She worked hard to learn the language and in-sisted that we speak English at home to help her. For almost the entire time our family lived in New York, even while my brother and I attend-ed grade school, my mother did not have a job. We're not sure what she did most of the day. When we came home from school, though, we al-ways had a snack and then a home-cooked meal a few hours later. And she made sure we did our homework every night.

Although she emigrated from Cuba in the early 1950s, before the Rev-olution, my mother shared some of the values of other later Cuban im-migrants with her children, particularly the importance of a good edu-cation and learning the language of their new country. When I stop to think about my work ethic, hustler mentality and wise ways with mon-ey, I realize they are not all that different than those of most Cuban Americans, or many other immigrant groups for that matter.

My mother had the extraordinary ability of squeezing fifteen or twenty cents out of every dime she had. Growing up in New York City, Lou and I somehow managed to have just about everything we needed be-cause she always got items at a steep discount or for free. Absolutely nothing, including food and clothes, was wasted in our home. She was resourceful enough to find the gifts I wanted most for Christmas, to get a good spot on Central Park West to watch the Thanksgiving Day pa-rade and obtain some tickets to see the Christmas show at Radio City Music Hall. Her thrifty way with money was a major reason why, years later, she and my stepfather were able to have two new houses built for them in New Jersey.

Born into an ordinary middle-class family in Cuba, Elena received an education typical for girls growing up in the Havana area during the 1940s. She did not have the kinds of special talent or skills that were in demand to be a nurse or teacher, and to the best of my knowledge, was not a waitress or domestic worker for other families like many immigrant women. After living a few years with her late father's family and completing school, Elena joined her mother in this country as a teenager. It was several years before the Cuban Revolution forced thousands of her compatriots to flee the island. She settled in the Upper West Side of Manhattan along with some other Cubans during the era depicted in the *Mambo Kings* book by fellow Cuban American Oscar Hijuelos and the subsequent movie adaption of the novel. My mother certainly wasn't wild and crazy, but she sure could dance. After her divorce from my father, I remember how she would practice dancing to Latin music on our record player with new boyfriends in our apartment living room. It was nice to see and amusing at times.

In her later years, after raising her family, my mother's jobs included being a clerk and a cashier. Despite her passion for pictures—I am eternally grateful for all the pictures she took and neatly organized in albums when I was young—my mother struggled with a digital camera, and never learned to use a computer.

My mother may not have seemed the warm, bubbly type of Cuban that Abuela Belen, Tía Gloria, and other women in my family growing up appeared to be. But Cuban she was and proud of it. In the absence of my father, she helped me appreciate Cuban culture, including its food and music. Cuban cuisine is a mix of Spanish and Caribbean food and bears little resemblance to Mexican food, as I've explained countless times during my life. I enjoyed the yellow rice and chicken and fried plantains that was a staple of our diet. I also liked eating the black beans and rice she regularly cooked for us, sometimes with thin flank steaks. When I returned from Cuba the last time, I often heard *"pachanga"* music coming from the speaker on our record player. It was a sound that originated in Cuba when my mother was a teenager and became very popular among Latinos in New York City shortly after she and my father married. One of the record albums I remember my mother often listening to when I returned from Cuba was *Pacheco y Su Charanga*, with its distinct black and orange cover laying nearby. My mother also enjoyed listening to the mambo sound of Tito Puente and other Latin dance music, much of which has its roots in the rhythms created by Caribbean slaves and is often referred to as "Afro-Cuban." At least once, my mother, brother and I rode a subway train uptown to see a Spanish-language movie starring the Mexican comic actor Cantinflas and watch Spanish-language singers perform on stage. I don't remember any of their names, but they were good!

Perhaps as a way to learn English and assimilate into her adopted country, I also remember my mother bringing home the 45 RPM singles "19th Nervous Breakdown" by the Rolling Stones, "Try Too Hard" by the Dave Clark Five, "Just a Little Bit Better" by Herman's Hermits and "Hang On Sloopy" by the McCoys to listen to on our record player while I was in fourth grade. Like many young women in the U.S. at the time, she loved the Beatles. In any case, she was largely the reason why I could identify myself as a Cuban American, despite letting my Spanish language skills erode and taking on the very non-Cuban surname of my stepfather during my teenage years.

My mother was considered an attractive young woman when we lived in New York City. With Abuela Belen's help, she was usually stylishly dressed whenever she stepped out of our apartment. Elena was slightly shorter than average and had an overbite, which is probably why she rarely smiled in photos taken in those days. But she had nice long brown hair and a slender frame accentuated by a full rear end that drew lusty comments from numerous smart-ass (no pun intended) Spanish-speaking men.

Among the things that impressed me about my mother was how she was able to enroll Lou and me in a Catholic elementary school at a time when the church did not allow parishioners to divorce. She rarely set foot inside the Church of Saint Paul the Apostle, which was attached to my elementary school, except for special occasions, like when Lou and I received our First Holy Communion. But my mother always insisted that the two of us go to church every Sunday morning and sit with our classmates. My identity as a Catholic was forged during those years as a Saint Paul's student and churchgoer. That identity felt particularly strong when I was in second grade and President John F. Kennedy was assassinated. My class was ushered into the church next door, and we all prayed for our fellow Catholic. Eventually, we were dismissed from church and stepped outside to see our grieving mothers and fathers. I recall feeling sad about how upset everyone seemed, even though I was only seven years old and too young to fully grasp the gravity of the tragedy. I remember our family spending part of the weekend at the Upper West Side apartment of Abuela Belen, who wept as a picture of President Kennedy hung on her wall. Years later, I learned that President Kennedy was not necessarily beloved by all Cuban Americans because of his role in the ill-fated Bay of Pigs operation in April 1961 and promise not to invade the country again during the Cuban Missile Crisis of October 1962. I did retain my identity as a Catholic for five more years, until my future stepfather insisted Lou and I become Lutherans like him.

Mom and Charlito

Chapter 3. The Young Boy: West Side Stories

One summer day in 1962 after I returned home from Cuba for the final time, my mother, brother, and I planned to visit Abuela Belen and Uncle John at their apartment. We walked to the subway station and while standing on the platform waiting for the train to arrive, I spat on the ground. A few moments later, I spat again. And again. Why? I don't know. But Lou looked at me quizzically, perhaps wondering where I learned this behavior since there were no subways in Havana, or anyone else in the station spitting. My mother began scolding me, basically telling me not to spit on subway platforms.

I quickly learned to respect and appreciate New York City's mass transportation system. Since our family had no car, we always rode a bus or subway train when we needed to go someplace that was more than just several blocks away. It helped that we lived just a few blocks from the Columbus Circle subway station, which was served by five train lines: the 1, A, B, C and D. From there, we could ride to many places in Manhattan as well as Brooklyn and the Bronx without switching trains. I liked to look out the front window of the first car and make believe I was driving the train. I enjoyed seeing how the tracks in front of me would sometimes curve and straighten as the lights from the next station became visible. When the train would pass red signal lights, I could sometimes see the train ahead of us on the same tracks.

When I wasn't traveling on the subway during the first year I returned from Cuba, I was pretending at home that I was. I liked to take an empty milk carton and glide it along the edge of the floor that met the walls in the hallway of our apartment, while mimicking the roaring and clacking beats of the subways I had become familiar with. While rapidly moving the milk carton and spitting out the associated subway sounds in our hallway, I would call out the stations the 1 train would stop at on the way to visiting my Abuela Belen and Uncle John: "72nd Street ... 79th Street ... 86th Street ... 96 Street." Many years later my mother told me how intense I seemed to be when playing like this in our apartment. She was also amused by the creative sounds of the subway that were emanating from her six- or seven-year-old son's mouth.

Within a few years, I had practically memorized the city's subway map. I could tell someone how to get almost anywhere in Manhattan and many other locations in the outer boroughs on the subway. Since almost every time I rode the subway while living in New York was to go someplace I wanted, I enjoyed being on trains. That positive association with subways has lasted my entire life. Even the sounds and smells of the subway, offensive to many riders, typically evoke pleasant thoughts for me. But I became a little disappointed well into my adult years when fewer and fewer trains had front windows to look out!

Years after I returned my mother recalled what a crude boy I had become during my last stay in Cuba. My skin was quite tanned and tough, my hair felt like straw, and my mannerisms were rather unpolished for someone who was about to be starting first grade in just a few weeks. I was neither Cuban nor American at that point. Rather, I was a six-year-old boy who was a rough mix of both. I didn't speak English, or at least the form of it that my Puerto Rican neighbors spoke. I also didn't speak the form of Spanish I heard from these same neighbors. It was frustrating.

This communication deficiency became apparent after I was at Saint Paul the Apostle School on 60th street between Columbus and Amsterdam avenues for a few days that September. My first-grade teacher thought I was deaf. She would speak to me like she did to her other students, and I would just stare back at her blankly. I could hear her just fine, actually. I just had no idea what she was saying. When our class stood in the direction of the American flag to repeat the words of the pledge of allegiance that she recited, nothing came out of my mouth. I only spoke Spanish at that point and had just returned home after my extended stay in Cuba. I had picked up only a few English words and phrases from Lou, who was perfectly bilingual, and they didn't sound like anything I heard in the classroom. My mother had somehow managed to enroll me in the school without anyone seeing or hearing me beforehand, probably because Lou was such a good student. When a school official contacted her after classes started, she said that I was not deaf but confessed I simply did not know the English language. I could have been taken out of the school—for the second year in a row after dropping out of kindergarten in Cuba the previous autumn—and forced to enroll in the public school just across 61st street from our Amsterdam Avenue home. Instead, the Catholic school kindly retained me.

Fortunately for me, my first-grade teacher was an exceptionally kind person. A nondescript woman who wore glasses and looked older than she was, I later learned she was an heiress to a large baked goods company. She had been sickly as a child, and in gratitude to God for her good health by the time she was a young adult, she had agreed to teach at a city parochial school for no pay. She also voluntarily tutored me and a few other classmates unfamiliar with the language on Saturday mornings that autumn. I remember those English-language classes. They began in our school classroom as she patiently taught us some basics. If the weather was good, the small group of us, which included my brother serving as a kind of teacher's assistant, would walk the few blocks to Central Park. During our stroll to and inside the park, the teacher would point out objects to us in English. At least once we were joined by her fiancé, a well-dressed dark-haired man who happened to be a Cuban American. By that Christmas, I was fluent in English and earning good grades in school, even as many of my Puerto Rican classmates continued to struggle with the language and schoolwork.

My mother was very proud of me as a student and on several occasions pointed out that, as a Cuban American, I was different than my classmates. I interpreted her comment to mean I was perhaps gifted with a sharper mind than most of my fellow Hispanics. It made me feel a little unusual but special at the same time. But I knew that some of my Puerto Rican classmates were smarter than me. One of them was a girl I befriended and would occasionally visit at her Amsterdam Houses apartment when her family was home.

"You were always so nice and well mannered, and I could tell that you were loved and well cared for," this classmate and friend recalled decades later. "For someone so young, you were smart and well-spoken, and seemed to get along with everyone. I remember your mother who reminded me so much of my own. She was a true lady with an innate grace and elegance who took pride in her children and in her role as their mother."

Saint Paul the Apostle School had a fascinating mixture of students during the 1960s. My classes at that time were typically large, with at least thirty and sometimes close to forty students. Many of us were Hispanics or Blacks from the Amsterdam Houses complex built shortly after World War II in what was known as the tough San Juan Hill neighborhood. A good number of our classmates, almost all Irish American or of continental European ancestry, lived in older tenement buildings just south of us in Hell's Kitchen. Unlike the Amsterdam Houses apartments where each unit had its own bathroom, those in the tenement buildings had only one bathroom per floor which a few families would share. At the other end of the spectrum were classmates, all of whom were white, who lived in pricey apartments around Central Park South. These students would typically start the school year with a new box of

64 Crayola crayons. I and other Amsterdam Houses classmates usually would have a new box of eight crayons in September. Classmates from the tenements rarely had a new box at all—often they would have just a few short or broken crayons.

Despite the diversity in our economic circumstances and ethnic backgrounds, my Saint Paul the Apostle School classmates generally got along well with each other. Kids being kids, there were occasional fights and shouting matches I assumed were normal for elementary school. But I don't think these altercations were typically based on our economic and ethnic differences. There were times during a week where my Amsterdam Houses classmates would go to both a wealthy friend's apartment and a poorer friend's home after school. These apartments were only a few blocks apart and we didn't think twice about it. But I don't believe, our Central Park South and Hell's Kitchen classmates regularly ventured into our Amsterdam Houses neighborhood, which was a little puzzling but not necessarily upsetting to me. Years later a friend told me that was because most of these white classmates of Irish or continental European descent were probably not comfortable in a predominantly Puerto Rican and Black neighborhood. That was too bad because, even though it was a public housing project, these classmates could have been able to more fully appreciate the nice planning work done by Grosvenor Atterbury, the accomplished architect of Amsterdam Houses. A former president of the Architectural League of New York who received a patent for prefabricated construction materials, he also helped design the renovated interior of City Hall and the American Wing of the Metropolitan Museum of Art, according to *The Encyclopedia of New York City*, edited by Kenneth T. Jackson and published in 1995.

There weren't many Cuban Americans in the Amsterdam Houses neighborhood when I was growing up there. I only remember one other family in the building next to mine. They seemed like a normal family with a working father, stay-at-home mother and two sons who attended Saint Paul's. It was during a social visit at their apartment that my mother, brother, and I first saw the Beatles on the Ed Sullivan TV show one Sunday night in the winter of 1964.

In New York City, Cubans have never comprised a sizable portion of the Hispanic population. By 1940, Puerto Ricans accounted for forty-six percent of the city's Spanish-speaking population, according to *The Encyclopedia of New York City*. That figure rose steadily to eighty-one percent by 1970. "Thus for several decades the city's Latin American community was synonymous with its Puerto Rican community," according to the encyclopedia, although "The number of Latin Americans from countries other than Puerto Rico increased during the 1960s after the Cuban Revolution (1959) and the Dominican civil war (1965) and was reflected in the growth of several Latin American neighborhoods in New York City." (Note to the fine encyclopedia's editors: Puerto Rico is not a country, but a U.S. territory.)

Most of my Hispanic neighbors and classmates were Puerto Ricans. I definitely felt a kinship with them, particularly since our parents spoke the same language and we enjoyed many of the same kinds of foods for dinner. But my mother often reminded me that we were not Puerto Ricans, but Cubans. I believe that may have been a way for her to help me feel special, but I knew it also reflected her unflattering view of many Puerto Ricans.

A Puerto Rican couple lived in the apartment next door to us. They had five children, the two youngest of which were theirs. The oldest three were hers from a previous marriage. I'm not sure how her second husband made his livelihood, but I did see him walk down Amsterdam Avenue more than once with a parrot perched on his shoulder. He also boxed, which along with his goatee, penetrating eyes and sly smile made him seem like a cool, tough Puerto Rican.

The Puerto Rican woman next door and my mother conspired on Christmas Eves to help keep Lou and me believing Santa Claus would arrive at our apartment only after we fell asleep. As we approached our apartment door after dinner at Abuela Belen's apartment, our neighbor would open her door and say that Santa Claus had not yet arrived, so we needed to get to bed as soon as possible. She was right—there were no gifts under our Christmas tree that night, but they were there the next morning!

I don't know who lived directly upstairs from me, but I know they loved Latin music. Many times when Lou and I laid down to sleep we would hear the sounds of Tito Puente and other Latin artists blare from the record player above our bedroom. It sounded good, and we often fell asleep with those beats in our heads.

Most of my other neighbors were Black, including the family on the opposite side of our apartment. I don't remember these neighbors ever smiling. I rarely talked to them; they seemed very serious all the time. The father and one or both of his sons sometimes stared out the hallway window with what seemed like tan-colored stockings on their skulls. It seemed unusual to me, so once out of curiosity I asked them about it. They explained it helped relieve their headaches. It was not until years later I was told my Black neighbors were probably using the stockings to flatten their hair.

I can only recall speaking to the Black woman next door once. She rang our doorbell one afternoon collecting donations for the March of Dimes. I quickly looked around our apartment for all the dimes I could find, and I gave her a few. She still didn't smile but I'm sure she said thank you.

My best friend during some of the time I lived in New York City was Kevin, a tall Black classmate who resided in the same Amsterdam Houses neighborhood. We shared interests in music and baseball, had some mutual school friends and enjoyed hanging out together. Sometimes we played records or watched baseball games in our apartments. On other occasions we spent time looking at or "flipping" baseball cards somewhere outside. We also liked to pass the time after school in a playground or just hanging out and talking with friends, some of whom were girls. But during the first three years after I moved out of the neighborhood I only saw Kevin twice. We went our separate ways, but I never forgot what a good friend he was and how nice his family was to me.

More than thirty years after we had last spoke, as the internet made finding old friends easier, I decided to search for him online. I came across several listings of his name, one of them in New Jersey. I called the telephone number I found online. The sound of his voice brought a big smile to my face, and joy to my heart.

"This is he," the voice replied when I asked if he was the same Kevin who went to grade school with me in New York during the mid-1960s. Then we talked about the stations our lives had passed through since we last got together. It was as if we were reconnecting after thirty-three days, not almost thirty-three years.

I learned Kevin had attended All Hallows High School in the South Bronx. Even though he didn't start playing basketball until he was finishing grammar school, he played well enough for his high school varsity team to earn a scholarship to Saint Joseph's College in Maine, where he was active in theater and graduated with a bachelor's degree in biology. He returned to New York and became an actor while also making sales calls to hospitals and eventually working as a laboratory technician, marrying, and moving to New Jersey.

We agreed to get together a few weeks later in the old neighborhood. I met his family and he met mine. I was particularly excited to introduce my youngest son to my kind and handsome friend who I named him after in fond memory of our childhood days. My son was also happy to meet this special person.

We visited our old playgrounds and walked past the apartment buildings where we had lived. When we stopped at the very spot where he had taught me how to play baseball, Kevin astonished me by pulling out of his pocket a self-portrait I had sketched and mailed to him shortly after moving to New Jersey.

In the years since our reunion, we have stayed in regular contact. We've met for coffee or tea several times, enjoyed a few basketball games, concerts, and taken a ferry ride to a baseball game. We hooked up at a reunion of former Saint Paul the Apostle School classmates in the church basement in 2004. Our families have gotten together for visits. Mostly, we've spoken on the phone about the ups and downs of our lives since our childhood days on the West Side of Manhattan. During one of our conversations in 2020, I learned his godfather was Cuban. Kevin told me that while his mother was in the hospital to give birth to him, she became friends with a Black woman from our neighborhood and church. This woman gave birth to a daughter who six years later would be a classmate of ours at Saint Paul's. The neighbor Kevin's mother befriended was married to a Cuban man, and they became his godparents.

Among the most interesting stories Kevin and I reminisced about of growing up in the Amsterdam Houses neighborhood involve Halloween. Trick-or-treating was a breeze for kids—those of us living in the 13-story buildings on Amsterdam Avenue could just walk up and down the stairway, knocking on doors on every floor, and get lots of candy without ever stepping outside. Kids being kids, of course, we just had to go outside to check out the costumes and other scenery around the neighborhood. Rumors would quickly circulate about an apartment or building that was particularly generous or interesting, and many of us would make our way there. But we also had to be wary of some of the older tough-looking kids who stole candy from young trick-or-treaters. These guys would walk around swinging stockings full of white chalk powder (or worse). They would threaten to beat kids with it to ruin their costumes and make them cough and rub their eyes until they were defenseless if they didn't surrender their candy. Lou, Kevin, and I tried to avoid these kids—not always successfully—and we still remember their names.

Kevin and I also recall an extremely tall teenager walking to and from Power Memorial Academy, located directly across Amsterdam Avenue from my building, around 1963-65. The tallest person I had ever seen at this point in my life, this Black teenager stood out as he walked from the Columbus Circle subway station, past Saint Paul the Apostle School and on Amsterdam Avenue in the morning, and back to the subway many late afternoons. A star basketball player at Power Memorial Academy, he was known as "Little Lewie" to many of my classmates and neighbors. When he graduated in 1965, he went on to attend the University of California at Los Angeles and led its men's basketball team to three national championships. He then became the National Basketball Association's all-time leading scorer while being a member of six NBA championship teams, earning six Most Valuable Player awards and a record nineteen NBA All-Star selections during a twenty-year professional career. Along the way, he converted from Catholicism to Islam and changed his name from Lew Alcindor to Kareem Abdul-Jabbar.

And I'll never forget the Great Northeast Blackout of November 9, 1965. It was a Tuesday afternoon and Lou and I were back home in our 10th floor apartment after school. I was a fourth grade student, and having acquired a passion for baseball a few months earlier, was reading a sports magazine with Los Angeles Dodgers pitcher Don Drysdale on the cover. The lights began flickering after five o'clock, and by 5:30 our apartment was dark. My mother, brother and I opened our door to go into the hallway to look outside. Neighbors were congregating there, and we were startled to see the New York City skyline to our south completely dark. The only lights were those of cars traveling north on Amsterdam Avenue. My mother managed to make us dinner that night as we stayed indoors in dark silence. The lights were back on the following morning, but I never found the sports magazine I was reading when the blackout began. It was truly a Twilight Zone moment in my life.

The most painful incident that happened to me while living in New York City was breaking my collarbone shortly after my eleventh birthday. Lou and I were playing ball with some friends in a grassy lot on 62nd Street just across Amsterdam Avenue from the back of our apartment building. Someone hit a high fly ball and I backpedaled slowly to catch it. But before I could, a big, heavy Puerto Rican neighbor and classmate charged full steam ahead from behind me to also try to catch the ball. Boom! The collision instantly cracked my collarbone and I writhed in pain. That was quickly followed by something almost as painful: My brother hit me in the rear end with a baseball bat, not believing I was actually hurt! I immediately went home, and my mother and I walked a couple of blocks to Roosevelt Hospital, where a doctor arched my shoulder back and then put my left side in a sling so that the broken collarbone could set properly. Since I was young, the collarbone healed quickly, and I never had a problem with it again. My mom and I were livid at Lou afterward and she gave my brother a beating. I do recall having lots of aches and pains that year for some unknown reason. Perhaps my brother, not normally prone to violence, simply thought I was being a bit of a hypochondriac.

Among my most pleasant memories of growing up in New York were the summer weekend days our family spent at Coney Island, Brighton Beach and Rockaway Beach. We always travelled to them by subway. The ride to Rockaway Beach was my favorite. It was fun to look out the window of the subway car as it slowly made its way over Jamaica Bay. Sometimes at the end of the day we would stop at Rockaway Playland to go on a few rides. For us, though, Coney Island was by far the best amusement park. Sometimes after enjoying the day on the sand and in the water at Brighton Beach or Coney Island, we would spend a couple of hours on rides and eat at the original Nathan's Famous on Surf Avenue. As an adult, I've never gone too many years without visiting Coney Island; I regularly rode the historic Cyclone roller coaster until I was in my early fifties. I also remember taking a bus across the Hudson River to the amusement park in Palisades Park in New Jersey with my mother, brother and Abuela Belen on my birthday. I smiled nonstop while enjoying the rides and walking around that evening wearing a button that read, "Hi! I'm 8 years old!"

Even though I was Cuban, my parents were divorced, and I lived in a neighborhood located smack in the middle of the biggest city in the U.S., I actually thought my life in New York between the time I was six and eleven years old was similar in many ways to those of lots of young kids around the country during the 1960s. Seriously! I went to a good school just a few blocks away and was a conscientious student. Our family always had a black-and-white television in our living room. I enjoyed watching cartoons, *Soupy Sales*, *The Chuck McCann Show*, Sonny Fox on *Wonderama*, *Officer Joe Bolton's Three Stooges Funhouse*, *Winchell-Mahoney Time*, re-runs of *Abbott and Costello*, *Laurel and Hardy*, *Our Gang* and, eventually, baseball games and premieres of *The Addams Family*, *The Munsters*, *Get Smart*, *Batman*, *Lost in Space* and *The Monkees* episodes on TV. I also watched *The Ed Sullivan Show* on some Sunday nights and, with my mom, Myrta Silva's variety TV show, *Una Hora Contigo* (An Hour with You), on Channel 47, which was the first local Spanish-language station.

My brother and I didn't want to stay inside our apartment any longer than necessary while growing up. We roller skated, went sledding after it snowed, played war games in empty lots, and passed the time on swings and slides in playgrounds and hanging out with friends in the neighborhood. We often played hide-and-seek, but two street games that were equally popular were skully (or skelly) and red light green light. We played skully almost anywhere a big square could be hand-drawn with twelve boxes on the interior perimeter and a 13th in the center. The object was to flick a small disk on the ground from the first to last box in sequential order before anyone else. Most of us used a bottle cap as our disk. The most serious players would use a glide, a heavier round metal piece which they would pry from the bottom of a school desk leg. In the red light green light game, one of us would have our back turned to the others and say, "red light green light, one-two-three" and then quickly turn around. If you were caught moving while advancing after he turned around, you were out. If you were able to advance enough to tag him without being caught moving, you won and would take a turn saying, "red light green light, one-two-three." By the time I was in fifth grade, I also started enjoying flirting with girls and listening to popular music on AM radio.

During 1966-67, my brother, friends and I learned to hustle for a little spending money. My most profitable hustle was opening taxicab doors for patrons at the Lincoln Center for Performing Arts. On some Saturdays, a small group of us would walk a couple of blocks to the Columbus Avenue side of Lincoln Center. While there, dressed in our normal street clothes, we would open the doors of the yellow cabs as they pulled up to the curb to discharge passengers before a matinee or evening performance. Most riders getting out of the cabs would simply ignore us as we held their door open. Some would tip us a quarter or other loose change. In less than two hours or by the time a policeman or security guard shooed us away, we would have a few dollars. That was plenty to buy a lot of baseball cards or even a record album.

Another hustle that was much quicker and about as profitable was fetching coins from the Columbus Circle fountain that was also just a few blocks from my Amsterdam Avenue home. On a few early evenings, we would scope out the fountain in the middle of the circle to see where the shiniest coins thrown in had settled. We would take off our sneakers and socks. Then, when there were few people around and the traffic had quieted, we would walk into the fountain for a minute or so to scoop up quarters, dimes, and nickels. A couple of dollars was a great haul in such a short time. A few of my friends also made some money carrying groceries home for elderly shoppers outside a supermarket on Ninth Avenue just south of our church and school. After doing it once, I didn't find it a good investment of my time.

Also living on the West Side of Manhattan were Abuela Belen and Uncle John. During our time in New York, my family would regularly take a subway or bus a couple of miles uptown to visit them. The five of us spent every Easter Sunday, Thanksgiving Day, and Christmas Eve together until my mother remarried. We also celebrated birthdays together. During summer weekends, the five of us would often go to Brighton Beach or Rockaway Beach for the day, sometimes to Coney Island. The five of us went to the World's Fair in Queens in 1964.

Some of my fondest childhood memories in New York involve Abuela Belen. She always prepared wonderful Cuban meals when we visited her, first in her apartment on 99th Street between Amsterdam Avenue and Broadway, then on the southeast corner of 101st Street and West End Avenue where she lived with Uncle John between 1964-1975. Eventually, she moved to 91st Street between Columbus and Amsterdam avenues and lived by herself for sixteen years before passing away in 1991. I loved her Thanksgiving dinners of turkey, black beans, and rice. Once when I was very young, I was impressed thinking she had managed to cook the turkey without breaking the egg it appeared to be laying while captured. It took a few minutes for me to realize she placed the egg by the turkey's butt before cooking it. I also remember how happy I was to see how well she looked the first time I visited her after she broke a leg while falling on a Broadway sidewalk. She was impeccably dressed and wore nice makeup as she chatted away with her leg in a cast, happy to see us.

I am eternally grateful for all the fine Cuban coffee Abuela Belen made me over the years. Cuban coffee is very strong. And like her, it is also very sweet. I once asked her affectionately, "*Abuela, ¿quieres un poco de café con tu azúcar?*" ("Grandma, do you want a little coffee with your sugar?"). To this day, I prefer the El Pico or Café Bustelo brands she always had around her apartment when I buy espresso coffee for my *café con leche* or *cafecito*.

After I had graduated from college, started my career and gotten married, Abuela Belen surprised me one day by giving me a ring that had belonged to her first husband. Abuelo Alberto passed away sixteen years before I was born. I only saw a couple of grainy black and white photos of him. He was a thin man with dark hair and a wisp of a mustache. His elegant white gold ring with diamonds and sapphire stone will forever link us. And it always reminds me of Belen's kindness.

In 2017, on the 70th anniversary of her arrival in the U.S., I wrote on my blog, *1400 Characters*, that Abuela Belen "was a widow and talented seamstress who came to the U.S. in search of a better life, like millions before and after her. She tried but could never master the English language like my mother did. She got most of her information from Spanish-language newspapers, magazines, radio and TV and her Spanish-speaking neighbors, friends, and co-workers in New York. She cared about her new country, and regularly voted in elections. She was one of the most inspirational people in my life, and a very loving sweet woman. And she was a good American."

Uncle John, Mom, the Young Boy, Abuela Belen, Lou

Chapter 4. The Nephew: Tio Abogado

Seeing Uncle John was usually among the highlights of visiting Abuela Belen when all of us lived in New York City during the first five years after I returned from Cuba for good. As with me and Lou, John's parents were divorced and he didn't have much of a relationship with his father, a Chilean immigrant who worked for years as a U.S. Merchant Marine. Like me, John inherited some of his father's physical features. Most notable were the light complexion, high cheekbones and nose often associated with Chileans that have some native Indian ancestry. But he was always slim like his mother and unlike his broad-shouldered, squatty father. John was only five years older than me and had a wild side to him along with an interesting collection of magazines and music albums. Lou and I did enjoy reading his Mad magazines and listening to his music, but mostly we just liked horsing around with him in the apartment. He sometimes liked to grab my hand and while repeatedly slapping my face with it ask, "Why are you hitting yourself?!?" He also helped me improve my English-language skills by once telling me, "It's not 'fot'—that's not a word—it's pronounced 'fart!'"

On weekends in the summer, he, my brother and I and our mothers would sometimes go to Brighton Beach or Rockaway Beach for the day. Uncle John would sometimes dig a hole in the sand and then cover it with newspaper and a thin coat of sand. The three of us boys would get a kick out of seeing some unsuspecting beachgoer step in the thin coat of sand and fall by the hole. One time a food vendor stepped in the covered hole and dropped some of the pretzels he was selling. My mother and uncle did not hesitate to help themselves to a pretzel before the vendor got back on his feet.

Like me, Uncle John had little contact with his father, my step-grandfather, as he grew up. He did not speak well of his father and was not pleased that he was at Abuela Belen's funeral in 1991. It was also clear to me early on that John and my stepfather did not like each other. It seemed my uncle did not particularly enjoy talking to my stepfather during our visits to see him and Abuela Belen. On the car ride home, my stepfather often passed judgments and complained about John, who Lou and I typically just had a good time seeing.

My uncle and I had some other, slightly less mischievous fun outside of his apartment as we got older. When my brother got married for the first time in 1974, John drove to the church near Bloomfield, New Jersey in an old Volkswagen Beetle. Part of the car's floor had rusted out, revealing the street underneath, but the two of us had some fun riding around town in the Beetle afterward anyway. Six years later, on the night after Lou got married for the second time on the Alabama property of his wife's family, John and I shared a tent in the backyard as our sleeping quarters. We had a blast trying to frighten each other with stories about scary creatures in the woods.

Around 1995, after he became a father of three children and I of two, we happened to be vacationing just a few miles apart in the Adirondack Mountains. Among the topics we discussed while together one afternoon was the Ebola virus that had originated in Africa and was spreading to other parts of the world. After a couple of hours together during which we got increasingly goofy, we drove a motorboat to the middle of a lake with our eldest children. Suddenly, the motor conked out. We pulled the starter chain a few times but could not get the engine going. "It's the Ebola virus!" Uncle John declared. "The motor has Ebola!" While rowing the boat ashore and for a few hours afterward, we got sillier and more creative with references to the Ebola virus. My wife said she never saw me laugh as much as I did that day. When we returned home, she bought a paperback book about the Ebola virus and suggested I keep it on my office desk. "Whenever you get stressed out, look at the book and remember how much fun you had with John that day," she said. Her idea worked. I kept that book on my office desk for a few years and relieved some stress by looking at its cover and thinking back to that afternoon in the Adirondack Mountains with my uncle.

I stayed close with Uncle John for the rest of his life, even as we raised our families, became immersed in our careers, and spent less and less time with each other. He and his family were the only ones from my mother or father's side of the family who were at my eldest son's wedding in July 2013. I will always remember what a great time he and Aunt Donna had with us that evening at the Loeb Boathouse in Central Park, just a couple of miles from their New York City apartment.

Uncle John had quite an interesting career. Actually, his twisting and turning journey through life included a series of careers. After graduating from a Catholic high school in 1969, he enrolled in Saint Francis College in Brooklyn. Two years later, he dropped out to travel to Mexico and elsewhere. He then worked a succession of jobs, including as an apartment doorman, handyman and taxicab driver, before completing his undergraduate studies. He landed a full-time job with the NYC Department of Social Services but quit after a year. He said he was tired of people begging for money and trying to game "the system." For some reason, even though years later family and friends recounted his poor sense of direction, John decided to become an air traffic controller. He went away to the Federal Aviation Administration academy in Oklahoma City for a few months of training and came back with a full-time position at a suburban New York airport. He held that job, which he often described as the most stressful he ever had, for less than two years. In August of 1981, two years after getting married to Aunt Donna and just a couple of months after he was a groomsman at my wedding, my uncle was among 11,345 members of the Professional Air Traffic Controllers Organization fired from their job for going on strike.

At that point, after observing how much income law firms were generating from the PATCO job action, Uncle John decided to go to law school. He was studying for his law degree when his first child was born. After graduating, he worked as an assistant district attorney in the Southern District of New York. He claimed it was the most interesting job he ever had. Eventually, he joined an insurance company as an in-house attorney and became a partner in the law firm that continued providing legal services to the company after it was spun off. It was around that time he began using "*tioabogado*"—Spanish for "uncle lawyer"—in his email address. I often recount Uncle John's succession of careers to young people who tell me they don't know what they want to do when they grow up.

The birth of Uncle John and Aunt Donna's first child, a baby girl, in 1985 was a major inspiration for me to become a parent. Knowing the bad experience he had with his father and the twists and turns of his career, I was glad to see how happy and well-adjusted he was to have a child to care for in his life. John and Donna had two more children, both sons, before their daughter turned nine years old. I've heard his children, whose ethnicities are half-Irish, quarter-Cuban and quarter-Chilean, referred to as "McCubans" by other family and friends!

Our shared experiences in our family's "gang of five" and as sons of estranged fathers who then prioritized fatherhood were among the reasons Uncle John was such an important figure in my life. Plus, he was among the most interesting, smartest, funniest, and hardest working guys I knew. Interestingly, some family members have told me they see a physical remembrance between me and John as I've gotten older. Certainly, our salt-and-pepper hair and moustaches are similar.

In 2015, Uncle John was diagnosed with cancer. In February of 2018, he mustered enough strength to be part of his daughter's wedding on a damp but enjoyable evening at the Liberty Warehouse in Red Hook,

Brooklyn. That September, John died in his home at the age of 67. I remain crushed by his passing.

I always brought a Mad magazine with me when I visited him during those last few years in the 101st Street and West End Avenue apartment he continued sharing with Aunt Donna after raising their three children. A few days after he passed away, I wrote on *Facebook* that cancer "will never take away memories of the many special moments he and I shared on this earth." I said he was one of only two men (Lou the other), "who was always there for me from the time I was born. He was never more than a phone call or short trip away to provide me advice or just a good laugh, often just minutes apart. I always treasured our times together."

Uncle John and the Nephew, 2013

Chapter 5. The Happy Camper: Breaths of Fresh Air

While we lived in New York City, our family never went on vacation. I do recall one of my mother's boyfriends, Felix, once taking the four of us for a couple of days to upstate New York. There, my brother and I visited the Baseball Hall of Fame in Cooperstown for the first time. We also stopped at Howe Caverns and a few other tourist attractions before returning home in the boyfriend's white Corvair. It was the last time my mother dated Felix, an older Puerto Rican divorcee who was soft-spoken, kind and patient with Lou and me. I wonder how different my life would have turned out if my mother had ended up marrying Felix. I'm sure he would have been a nice stepfather and taken good care of my mother, brother, and me. I don't think my mother was truly attracted to him or loved him, but she appreciated how nice and unselfish he was with us.

Instead of family vacations, my mother arranged for Lou and me to be away for a couple of weeks every summer at no cost as part of the Fresh Air Fund program. *The New York Herald Tribune* sponsored the program for decades into the 1960s. The program still exists today. Typically, Lou and I along with dozens of neighborhood children and many others from around the city would travel by bus from midtown Manhattan or by train from Penn Station to a "friendly town" in suburban New Jersey or rural Pennsylvania. There, a family would host us for two weeks. The communities I was sent to and families that hosted me were radically different than what I was used to in New York. That was, and still is, the concept behind the Fresh Air Fund program. For me, it was a different world, with more green grass and less noise and people. And to my host families, this boy from New York City must have been different from the kids around their community.

I enjoyed nearly all my Fresh Air Fund vacations with families outside of New York City between 1963-67. The families I stayed with typically had children my age and hoped we would all get along and have fun for a week or two. That was certainly the case with a family that hosted me in a western suburb of Harrisburg, Pennsylvania when I was about nine years old. Their kids were active and liked to play baseball and read comics. They made me feel welcome, and as a reward for being a bat boy at one or two of their Little League games they gave me my first baseball cap to take home. The red and white hat was embroidered with the letters W and H, which stood for West Hanover.

My best Fresh Air Fund experiences, in 1966 and 1967, came right after the only time I remember being poorly matched with a family. A Bergen County, New Jersey couple that hosted me hoped I would be a good playmate for their only son. The boy was a few years younger than me and badly "spoiled." He didn't want to do things a ten-year-old boy, at least one from New York City like me, enjoyed, which were usually games and other physical activities outside. And I didn't really want to do the things he liked, which always seemed to be passive and inside the house. He whined and cried a lot, and within a week his mother realized I was not going to work out as her son's playmate. I was taken to another host family, which already had a Fresh Air Fund boy plus five children of their own. I had a great time with the six other children that week.

The following summer, the same family invited me and the other Fresh Air Fund boy back to stay with them for two weeks. We had an even better time together. The kids taught me to ride a bicycle and treated their two New York City visitors as friends. I never forgot the kindness of that family. We exchanged letters for a while afterward and, many years later while I was a college student, I drove to Hillsdale, New Jersey, and paid them a visit.

I also remember early on in my Fresh Air Fund experience staying with a young childless couple who lived in a trailer home in the middle of a field. The man was away at his job during the day but would toss a baseball and play with me when he returned home in the late afternoon. I spent most of the time with his wife playing board games, visiting family and friends, and going to other places in the area. I don't know why they wanted to host me. At times I felt bored and restless. I hope their experience with me didn't discourage them from eventually having children of their own.

Along with sending New York City kids to host families outside the city, the Fresh Air Fund also provided the opportunity to go to a sleep-away camp in Dutchess County in upstate New York. (Note: As a boy, I thought any place in New York State north of the city was "upstate." Many people still do!) I did that only once when I was about eight years old. It was the first time my brother and I were together for a Fresh Air Fund vacation, and we didn't care for it much. It was just too "rustic" for us at the time to stay in a "lean-to" shelter, with its open front, for two weeks. Some of the activities at the camp were more fun than others. I learned to swim, but not well enough to pass the swimming test at the end of the camp session. The food was, at best, mediocre.

That summer, at Camp Marks Memorial in Dutchess County, I met the tall, young, blond, light-complexioned man who would eventually become my stepfather. Although Lou and I never went back to the camp, I corresponded with my future stepfather for over a year. He was not my counselor or village leader at the camp, but I was among the handful of campers he stayed in touch with during the following year. At that point, I had never corresponded with anyone else I met at a Fresh Air Fund camp. I was flattered by this twenty-one-year-old man's interest in me.

My future stepfather came to my family's New York City apartment to visit me around Christmas 1965. A few months later, he returned to take me, my brother and mother out to a baseball game at Yankee Stadium. He and my mother began dating regularly shortly afterward, often at Rockaway Beach or Brighton Beach with Lou and me in tow. My mother was very happy that this young, educated man with a steady job enjoyed being with her and her children. She thought he was handsome, and he was certainly younger than any man I remember her dating after I returned from Cuba.

Indeed, my mother and future stepfather were an odd couple. He turned twenty-three years old in August of 1966, the same month my mother turned thirty. She preferred to keep her age to herself and sometimes said she was a year or two younger. My future stepfather had led a relatively sheltered life. He lived with his parents and attended the same Lutheran church in the suburban New Jersey town of Bloomfield where he had been baptized. He stayed at home while attending college and starting his career as a teacher. It was quite a contrast to the life my mother had led at that point as a Cuban immigrant in New York City, Roman Catholic and, more recently, a divorcee and parent of two growing children. My brother and I could understand my mother's interest in a younger, responsible man who enjoyed the company of school-age children. But we could not quite comprehend his interest in our mother. Frankly, I thought it made more sense for him to pursue a relationship with a younger, single, attractive Chilean friend of my mother. When this woman met my future stepfather, they showed some interest in each other. In any case, my mother and future stepfather got engaged by Christmas of 1966 after dating for about six months. They were married in January of 1967 and the rest, as they say, is history ... a history in which my identity's journey took some sharp twists and turns.

The Happy Camper's First Holy Communion

PART 2: "Charley ... what ?!?"
Chapter 6. The Outcast: A Stepfather and New Town

In the fall of 1967, when I was eleven years old and a sixth-grade student, I told my friends in New York City I was moving to "the country," to a place in New Jersey called Bloomfield. After spending all my elementary school years on the northern fringe of Hell's Kitchen, in "the projects" formally known as Amsterdam Houses, our new family was relocating across the Hudson River to my stepfather's hometown. This was so he could be closer to the school in Newark, New Jersey where he taught.

Lou and I weren't sure why we needed to relocate. Just five months after our mother and stepfather had married, we moved to a bigger apartment in the same building. That autumn, my mother gave birth to another son. I was happy attending Saint Paul the Apostle School and enjoying the friendship of my classmates. Lou was attending Monsignor William R. Kelly School, a magnet school just over a mile away, and seemed well adjusted in the company of other bright students. Abuela Belen and Uncle John, the two other most important people in my life at the time, lived just a short ride away on the Upper West Side.

My stepfather was a fourth-grade teacher in Newark. During the school year in 1967, he drove his 1966 Ford Galaxie against New York City rush hour traffic to and from his New Jersey school. After living in his parents' suburban New Jersey house, it was often a challenge for him to fall asleep in our apartment. He often had a hard time getting up in the morning to make it to his school on time.

"How can you sleep through the night with the noisy fire trucks on Amsterdam Avenue?" my stepfather asked my mother, Lou, and me one morning shortly after he moved in with us. My brother and I looked at each other, puzzled, and I replied, "What noisy fire trucks?" To us, the sounds around the firehouse a few blocks from our apartment were just background noise, part of the soundtrack that was life in the city. We were used to the fire trucks and police sirens, and they didn't keep us awake. Neither did the music from our Puerto Rican neighbor's record player directly above our bedroom. To the contrary, it helped us fall asleep.

My brother and I began sensing our blue-eyed, blond-haired German American stepfather was feeling uneasy in our largely Black and Puerto Rican neighborhood as our first months together rolled by. Besides the commute to work, parking his car in our neighborhood became an issue for him. He always managed to find a spot on the street, but he was concerned when he wasn't able to keep an eye on it. He feared it might get broken into by a drug addict or stolen by a car thief.

We learned a lot about our stepfather that first year. Within a few months of his marriage to our mother, he started expressing strong, mostly negative, opinions about our neighborhood, our schools, our church, and even extended family members. He started making fun of us, referring to Lou and me as "the nut and the butt," "the queer and the rear," "the odd and the end." (Apparently, he thought Lou was strange and I had a fat ass.) He also started ridiculing my mother, who was seven years older than him, for taking so long to walk across Amsterdam Avenue while she was pregnant with their child. After she cut her hair, he referred to her as "Georgy Girl," a not-so-flattering reference to a dowdy female in a popular song and film.

That first summer with our stepfather wasn't entirely without humor for me and Lou. One afternoon when our stepfather was having lunch with us, my mother prepared chicken noodle soup and placed the bowl down on the table in front of him while he was making his sandwich.

He was scraping his spoon across the bottom of a mayonnaise jar and poked at it so hard at one point that the bottom broke clean off, landing in his bowl of hot soup! My brother and I laughed. When he looked up at us with an angry scowl, we paused for a second, then laughed some more. Our stepfather was beside himself with anger as the broken glass with traces of mayonnaise sat in the soup bowl beside his unfinished sandwich. Lou and I laughed at the sight for a few more moments before we realized our stepfather would never find humor in the situation.

Even with our stepfather's attempts to put us all down, my brother and I were happy to have him in our lives at first. Our mother and biological father divorced before we started school and the few times we saw him every year were unpleasant. Our father rarely provided any kind of child support, and we quickly wound up on the welfare rolls, receiving public assistance. We basically grew up fatherless until our mother remarried.

Despite his low salary as a non-tenured teacher, our stepfather immediately assumed financial responsibility for basic expenses like the rent and food for our family. But in return, he expected all of us to treat him like a savior and constantly express our gratitude. It was soon obvious that his feelings and opinions were paramount.

One evening during the first summer with our stepfather, Lou and I went out to take a walk and buy some baseball cards. It was something we often did during summer nights, especially when the weather was nice, friends were around the neighborhood and a new series of Topps baseball cards were available in stores. After an hour or so, we returned home with our new baseball cards in hand, excitedly talking about some of the players we just got while chomping on pieces of the mediocre gum that came inside the packs of cards. Scowling, our stepfather asked us to come closer to him so he could smell our breath. Lou and I looked at each other, confused and a bit stunned.

Apparently satisfied his eleven- and twelve-year-old stepsons had not been drinking alcohol or smoking marijuana, which is all I could think of being the issue, he asked if we had brought any gum for him to chew. He had never asked us this before, even though we had already bought dozens of nickel packs of cards with gum by that time of the year. We said we had not, and told him we threw out most of the sticks of gum that came with the baseball cards since they tasted bad compared to Bazooka bubble gum that sold for only a penny a piece.

"Oh," our stepfather replied, acting wounded. Lou and I exchanged glances, wondering if we were bad stepsons for not thinking of him as we excitedly opened our new card packs and discarded the enclosed gum sticks. But we also wondered what was wrong with our stepfather. Ultimately, it was another reminder of how our family needed to be about him and his feelings. He expected us to always be thinking of him and constantly express our gratitude for his presence in our lives.

Around the same time, my brother and I noticed how easy it was to appear to hurt our sensitive stepfather in situations that were seemingly not about him. My mother heard that our biological father was working in a midtown Manhattan café and wanted to see his children. It wasn't often he asked for us to visit him, so my mother agreed. She asked our stepfather to drive us to the café. After a short and eerily quiet ride, Lou and I spent about an hour at the café counter while our father prepared short orders and talked to us. As usual, it was not a pleasant visit. When our stepfather's car pulled up in front of the café, we said our goodbyes and left.

Inside the car, our stepfather's long face awaited us. As he drove home, he complained we had not kissed him goodbye when we had stepped out of the car an hour earlier. He also said he was hurt that we seemed happy to be visiting our father. Yet again, Lou and I looked at each other, confused and a bit stunned. But this time we knew we had done nothing wrong. It was just the latest example of how nearly everything in our lives had to revolve around him. To placate him, we apologized. But we seethed inside.

So, even though Lou and I weren't sure why we needed to leave our New York neighborhood, we began to sense living in Bloomfield might be advantageous for our stepfather. In any case, we needed to embrace the change in order to satisfy him.

My brother's first memory of Bloomfield was the graffiti on the walls of a highway underpass. I remember the bird poop in that same area. This was "the country" we were moving to with our family. Despite these first impressions, our first visits in 1967 to the town that would become our new home were pleasant. We visited our stepfather's parents in the Brookdale section of town a few times. They were very nice to us and immediately treated us like their grandchildren. Lou and I quickly took a liking to them, but then and over the next few years these visits had an awkward, uncomfortable dimension to them.

They were difficult because our stepfather forced us to lie to his parents about our ages.

Our stepfather was afraid that his parents would disapprove of their twenty-three-year-old son's marriage to a divorcee who was much older than him and with two school-age children. To soften the situation, he told them my mother was only five years older than him. If that were true, however, it would mean that she would have given birth to her sons when she was just sixteen and seventeen years old. So, to make the situation believable to his parents, our stepfather told Lou and me to say we were a year younger than we actually were. And he told us to say we had both skipped a grade in school because we were such good students. We didn't quite understand why such lies were necessary, but we needed to embrace them in order to satisfy our stepfather. Later, my brother courageously ended this ruse by telling our step-grandparents the truth when we were (really) sixteen and fifteen. I was disappointed Lou did this without consulting me, but the relief of not having to lie about my age any longer overshadowed this disappointment. I also felt bad about the grudge my stepfather held for some time against my brother for exposing his lie.

Another struggle Lou and I had to contend with as we anticipated living in Bloomfield was a new surname. Our stepfather decided that we should begin using his last name, Bruns, rather than one we had been born with, Lopez. For many years I wondered if he felt using his surname would protect us from harassment in a town where there were hardly any Hispanics. (He once suggested I describe myself as half-Cuban and half-German, but I already knew who I was and what I wasn't.) I also recognized that since he was the head of the household and our father figure, he felt it only appropriate we begin using his surname. In hindsight, since he did not pursue a legal adoption or name change, it made no sense for him to feel entitled to make us change our last name to his. It proved awkward for us to explain to school officials and others that we were actually named Lopez but wished to be referred to as Bruns. It remained awkward until my brother and I legally changed our names after turning eighteen. During these years, my mother had her own difficulties and seemed indifferent to our plight.

When I first arrived in Bloomfield at eleven years old, my life was about to be turned upside down as I left my New York City neighborhood, school, church, and friends behind. And, it seemed, my identity as well. I was moving with my family to live in the suburbs in the south end of Bloomfield, in a two-family house on North 15th Street, and enroll in a new school, Carteret School, and go to a new church, Saint John's Lutheran Church. Worse, I would meet new people who would call me by a new name. It was not quite country living, I soon learned. But I was determined to focus on the positive and take on the challenge.

I entered Carteret School on Grove Street on December 4, 1967, a few days after saying good-bye to my New York friends and moving to our new Bloomfield home. My stepfather and I walked into the school office that morning to complete all the necessary paperwork and discuss our situation, including the difference between the name on my old school records and the one I would be using in this new school. The women in the office seemed a little perplexed but the principal was very understanding. He welcomed me to the school and escorted me to my new class.

A number of things struck me when I walked into the classroom for the first time. First, I was surprised by how small the class was. There were fewer than two dozen students in the room, which was a lot less than the sixth-grade class I left behind in New York City. I also noticed that everyone was wearing different clothes, unlike the Catholic school I came from where we all wore navy blue and white uniforms. And there were no Black or Latino-looking kids in the room.

I don't think I had ever been in a public setting where everyone in the room was white until that moment.

A few students smiled as I took my seat, but most of my new classmates simply took a very quick look at me. A few kids talked to me that day, but mostly they ignored me. I couldn't blame them. It was a gray Monday in the middle of the school year. As last-year students in the elementary school, they already had established friends and plenty of schoolwork to focus on.

When it was time for lunch recess, I walked half a mile back to my new home, quickly ate a sandwich and spoke with my mother about my new school. I then walked half a mile back and arrived in the schoolyard just minutes before the recess bell rang and students lined up with their class to return to their room. This pattern continued for all the seven months I attended Carteret School. Since I had one of the far-thest walks from school and back, I never had much time to talk or play with my new classmates during lunch recess. Sometimes on walks to and from my new school that winter, I talked to myself. I babbled as if I were a disc jockey on the New York radio station 77 WABC. (Most of the kids on my new street attended a Catholic school in Newark a few steps closer to our home, but my stepfather never discussed the possi-bility of going to that school with me.)

Something else that made me feel less than welcomed during my first days at Carteret School was my rejection by the musical director who was preparing for the annual Christmas show later that month. When I first met her, she had me audition by singing a few notes. Apparently concluding my voice was hardly that of a musical prodigy, she did not ask me to participate in any of the remaining rehearsals. So, I sat aside by myself while she directed my new classmates on stage through final preparations for the show. I was heartbroken. I had participated in a musical performance at Saint Paul's and thought of myself as at least av-erage in that regard. I also had a passion for popular music on the radio and was crushed that my new school's musical director hadn't thought enough of my voice to stick me somewhere in the choir where it could simply blend in.

That first winter in Bloomfield, I felt like an outcast. From my perspec-tive, my new classmates must have noticed I didn't dress as well as them. Perhaps they also thought I talked and acted differently. After years of being in my element in the city, with lots of like-minded friends, I felt like I didn't fit in with my Carteret School classmates. Like the boy in our class who was made fun of for having big ears—the only kid who befriended me those first months—and another boy ridiculed for having a "pug" nose, and the oversize girl with the Southern accent, I felt like I was an outcast among my classmates and not part of the "in crowd" at Carteret School. It was a very cold winter. My stepfather and mother did not seem to notice what Lou and I went through that first winter in Bloomfield.

Something else that struck me during those first months living in Bloomfield was the overt racism among a number of my new classmates and neighbors, almost all of whom were Italian American. I heard the words "nigger" and "spic" spoken more times in those months than I had during my entire life up to that point. I was introduced to the term "shine," and ridiculed for not knowing it was a reference to Blacks. I told some of my new classmates about the diverse group of friends I had left behind in New York City and it seemed to just give them another reason not to like me. When I talked to my stepfather about this, he rationalized it by explaining that people in the south end of Bloomfield felt threatened by the Newark riots the previous summer.

Another deflating classroom experience during those first months in Bloomfield involved a social studies project. While studying Bolivia, our class was assigned to create a small replica of a hut Incan Indians typically lived in. I had never undertaken such a project in New York City, but after consulting with my stepfather, I got some milk cartons and cardboard and, using scissors, glue, crayons, and sticks, put together a crude hut. It turned out to be very crude compared to the masterpieces made of plaster, ceramic and papier mâché that classmates had worked on with a great deal of help from their parents. I was humiliated on the morning all the students brought in their projects to display in the back of the room. Shortly afterwards, when my stepfather attended an after-school meeting in the room, he told me how embarrassed he, as a schoolteacher, felt seeing my crude little hut next to the others. Obviously, I didn't really need to hear that since I had been feeling that same embarrassment every day in class.

Despite feeling like an outcast among my classmates and struggling with mathematics (and craftwork) I had never been exposed to in New York City, I held on to my confidence and kept my chin up those first months in Carteret School. I was confident enough, actually, to challenge a bigger classmate who exchanged cross words with me to a fight. And I kept my chin up just enough for him to punch it and beat the crap out of me in the playground after school.

My classmates were shocked that I had challenged this other student to a fight. Some of them must have thought I was crazy or just plain stupid. Perhaps others were impressed at how fearless and cocky I seemed, maybe thinking this New York City kid was a great street fighter. Unbeknownst to them, I more than held my own in the few brawls I was in during my time in the city. But this fight was no contest. Moments after I raised my fists, my classmate punched me with his right fist and then his left. I was on the ground within seconds. He jumped on top of me and punched me some more before realizing I was in no shape to hit him back. He stood up and walked away triumphantly, our classmates seemingly satisfied that he had upheld the school and neighborhood's honor against this outcast from New York City. I licked my wounds as I walked home with my only friend, the boy often ridiculed for his big ears, dissecting what had gone wrong. (By the way, when my family moved again two years later and new classmates challenged me to fights, I beat the crap out of them.)

To their credit, my classmates began treating me with a little more respect afterward. And the boy who beat me up was kind to me from that moment on. It was a learning experience—I realized that being myself did not have to involve having a chip on my shoulder about losing a way of living I had been comfortable with. Instead, I learned I should be more open-minded to understanding new ways and different people. I had been this way, after all, growing up in New York City and dealing with lots of changes and different people year after year. And perhaps my classmates learned the lengths I was willing to go to be respected and accepted by them after standing up for myself.

As winter turned to spring in 1968, things started warming up for me both inside and out. Our class would sometimes go out to the playground during school hours, and I enjoyed running around with my classmates. By that point, one of the popular sixth-grade girls who I reconnected with on *Facebook* and at a reunion years later, recalls I seemed to "fit right in" after being a quiet new classmate. She did not know I was Cuban American until decades later.

"You had that bushy fall in your face bangs (hair). Very cute, personable, and good at sports. Very special smile too," my former classmate wrote. "I can still see you running around the playground playing baseball/softball, taking a whack at the ball that went far into the air."

My classmates learned I could field and throw a ball and, perhaps, was just a normal sixth-grade kid rather than an alien from New York City. But playing Little League baseball that first spring in Bloomfield provided another lesson. I learned how bad I was at trying to hit a fast-pitched baseball.

I had never played real baseball until I moved to New Jersey and joined the Bloomfield Southern Little League. In New York City I had played Wiffle ball and, of course, stickball. My friends and I had also played softball in playgrounds and sometimes on the dirt and grass fields of Central Park. I was good enough in those games that, shortly after I began following the Yankees and Mets on TV, I dreamed of becoming a major league baseball player. Those dreams died that first spring in Bloomfield.

The classmate who had beaten me up was a Little League teammate, but things between us were fine by this point. Sometimes, my stepfather would even drive the two of us boys to or from a baseball practice.

I got along fine with all my teammates, few of whom attended Carteret School.

The only Cuban American I met during my first two years in Bloomfield was my Little League team manager, Hector. It's possible he chose me for his team because of the Lopez surname on my birth certificate, which I needed to show league officials to register to play that season. I don't know if Hector had been born in Cuba or the U.S., but he spoke English without an accent. I also heard him speak fluent Spanish with my mother. When he managed our team, Hector had a short haircut and looked like a working-class man in his twenties. When I last saw him three years later, Hector had been sitting on a bench on Broad Street near Bloomfield Center, barefoot, with long hair and a button on his jacket that read, "Support Your Local Police and Keep Them Independent." I hardly recognized him. I don't think he recognized me. Nor do I believe he was managing Little League teams any longer by that point.

Preseason practices led me to believe I would play a lot despite my inexperience in hardball games. But my season began to go downhill before it even started when I was hit by a pitch during a practice game. The fastball hit my ribs just under my armpit, and it hurt like hell. I was one of the few players not issued a regular uniform by the start of the season, and I was not in the starting lineup when regular games began. I always struck out when I came off the bench late in games, which made it difficult for the manager to justify putting me in the starting lineup even though I was among the oldest players on the team (contrary to what my new step-grandparents thought).

Finally, late in the season, I began to hit the ball. I even hit a double that reached the chain link fence in the outfield during our next-to-last game, which made my teammates and me deliriously happy. We finished the season in last place, winning only four out of sixteen games, but by the time it ended I felt like I belonged on the team and, perhaps, in the town. Unfortunately, I did not play organized baseball for another two years. Because of the lie about my age, my stepfather did not allow me to sign up to play Babe Ruth League baseball the following spring. I had to tell his parents and my new friends I was not interested in playing baseball again, which was the furthest thing from the truth, of course.

As the school year and Little League season wound down, I was pleasantly surprised when a popular girl from another elementary school in the south end of Bloomfield, Watsessing School, invited me to a barbecue party. We had only met once, but she was a friend of a Sunday School classmate of mine at Saint John's Lutheran Church. The classmate had a crush on me and probably asked her to invite me. My Carteret School and Little League mates were even more surprised than me that I was invited.

Unfamiliar with Bloomfield streets that were not on my way to Carteret School, I asked my stepfather where the Evergreen Avenue location of the party was. I rode the blue second-hand bicycle I had received for Christmas for two miles toward the house I thought was around the Little League field. And I got lost. At one point, after asking a pedestrian for directions, I wound up on Evergreen Place in East Orange. I returned home and told my Sunday School classmate the next day—and my Carteret School and Little League teammates on Monday—that I simply couldn't find the house. They probably didn't believe me.

By the end of spring, after attending services and classes at Saint John's Lutheran Church for a few months, my brother and I made another realization: There really didn't seem to be much difference between the Roman Catholic and Lutheran religions. It was true we weren't permitted to take Holy Communion at Saint John's until we completed two years of confirmation studies. And we noticed that the pastor of the church, in contrast to the priests at Saint Paul's, was married with a family. From our perspective, those were the most significant differences in the religions. So, we couldn't understand why our stepfather was always critical of the Catholic church and why he felt we needed to switch religions when we moved from New York City. But it was a change we needed to embrace in order to please him. Fortunately, my new step-grandparents and other church members made us feel welcome in their place of worship on the corner of Liberty Street and Austin Place.

Summer finally arrived and I was eager to learn my way around my new town's streets. Lou and I regularly rode our bicycles around the area, discovering the neighborhood in the Watsessing School neighborhood that had previously stumped me. We also rode around the Berkeley and Fairview school neighborhoods near South Junior High School, which my brother transferred to after our move to Bloomfield and I would attend that fall. We ventured into Bloomfield Center. Sometimes we even crossed invisible borders into Newark and East Orange and noticed we were the only light-skinned people around.

I also became familiar with the streets of my new neighborhood by soliciting customers for a *TV Guide* magazine delivery route I established. Lou and I quickly learned that a twenty-five-cent monthly allowance from our stepfather wasn't going far. We thought it was so insignificant, we never accepted a penny from him. My brother began delivering the *Independent Press*, which was Bloomfield's weekly newspaper, every Thursday. Since I was too young to do that, I responded to a *TV Guide* advertisement and found twelve families who agreed to have me deliver a *TV Guide* to their doorsteps at the end of every week. It was good while it lasted, but the *TV Guides* were increasingly mailed to my home too late for customers to receive them from me before Saturday morning. Consequently, my customer base dropped below the threshold (ten) that *TV Guide* said I needed to maintain my business.

Besides not being broke, Lou and I were also determined to not be bored, which had never been an issue during our summers in the city.

We frequented Milbank Park on North 17th Street and sometimes Felton Field on Floyd Avenue that first summer in Bloomfield. Often, we played on our street with neighborhood peers who were fighting boredom without straying far from home. When it rained, I stayed indoors with my baseball cards, magazines, sports on TV and music on the radio, just as I had the previous summer when necessary.

I missed my New York City friends, often thinking about what they were up to and sometimes exchanging letters with them. I also missed the Hillsdale, New Jersey family I had spent a few weeks with the previous two summers, thanks to the Fresh Air Fund program. The irony of living in New Jersey, seemingly part of the way towards Hillsdale, yet feeling further away, was not lost on me. Nor was a growing unhappiness with a father figure that I (and all boys, I assumed) had always wanted in my life.

Occasionally on evenings that summer, I would accompany my stepfather on his part-time job delivering for a Chicken Delight franchise in East Orange. He would use his Ford Galaxie to bring dinners to customers in East Orange, Orange and, sometimes, West Orange. Rather than take the time to hunt for a spot to park his car by a customer's home, my stepfather would often leave me in his double-parked car with the other dinners to be delivered. I confess I sometimes pulled a French fry or two or three from these other dinners to supplement the increasingly tasteless and unfulfilling meals we were being fed at home. My mother tried to cater to my stepfather's dietary preferences on a modest budget at the time so they could buy a house as soon as possible.

When I shared these stories of my last year in New York City and first year in New Jersey with another family member and friends decades later, they asked how I could recount these experiences with such little emotion. After giving the question some thought, I realized that I suppressed most of my emotions during that part of my life. I knew that in our family at the time, only my stepfather's feelings mattered. In his eyes, my mother Elena, Lou, and I needed to only care about his feelings, because after all, he was earning the money for our family and providing for our basic needs. We were not allowed to do or say anything that might upset him.

The few times I did express strong emotions to my stepfather shortly after moving to Bloomfield led to major confrontations that ended with him taking offense. I was accused of being selfish or ungrateful for all he had done for me. He would hold a grudge against me for days, weeks, sometimes months. After one such confrontation, he said he would forgive me if I acted "extra special nice" to him. He then proceeded to regularly rate my behavior against this standard. In other words, he expected me to kiss his ass to get back into his good graces.

So, I basically learned to suppress my emotions to keep my stepfather off my back. My mother and brother did the same and it scarred them both for many years. I've largely recovered as I've raised my own family and thought more closely about my past. But the scar sometimes shows through when I think and tell stories about this period in my life with relatively little emotion.

After Labor Day 1968, I started attending South Junior High School. It was a huge school and most seventh graders like me were meeting classmates for the first time. I actually liked it. Many of the students in my homeroom apparently liked me enough those first weeks to elect me as their representative on the student council.

For the first few weeks at South Junior High School, I enjoyed sitting with some classmates during our lunch period. The problem was that after forty-five minutes, I was still hungry. While my classmates usually enjoyed a fresh and flavorful lunch from home, or at least a filling hot meal from the cafeteria that could be purchased for less than fifty cents, I had to make do with a skimpy sandwich that my mother had packed for me that morning. These lunches were not only inferior to those of our classmates, they were worse than the institutional lunches my brother and I used to get at our New York City schools. We asked our mother for better lunches, but our pleas fell on deaf ears as she and my stepfather continued to prioritize saving money to buy a house.

We decided to take matters into our own hands by getting jobs during our lunch periods selling milk to our classmates as they walked in and then cleaning their trays as they left. In return, Lou and I received a free hot meal from the cafeteria every day. We had only fifteen minutes to eat, which was just enough time if we downed our food quickly. Working during the lunch period cost us some social standing among our classmates, but we figured it was a fair price to pay for what was sometimes our best meal of the day. Our stepfather and mother were pleased to save a few cents and the effort of providing lunches to two growing boys and seemed to not care what it cost us in terms of social status with our peers.

My stepfather's fear of the "hippie" culture and our family's financial priorities—he and my mother remained determined to buy their own house in town within a year—prevented me from having anything as fashionable as a Nehru jacket or bell-bottom pants. Even a barber's haircut was beyond the family budget. My mother used to pay $1.00 or $1.50 for Lou and me to get a haircut from a Spanish barber near our school and church when we lived in the city. After she remarried, my stepfather bought a barber's electric clipper and began cutting our hair when he thought it was getting too long. Lacking experience or patience, he did not do a good job. Despite being fortunate to have thick, dark hair, it was uneven in length and difficult to comb into anything fashionable during the years my stepfather cut it. When I started delivering newspapers to make decent money, I began walking to a barber shop in the North Center on Broad Street for haircuts and paid for them myself.

Despite my clothes and hair and other obstacles, I felt like I fit in with my peers at South Junior High School. I made many new friends and was earning the good grades I had normally received as a student in New York City. For the first time since moving to Bloomfield nearly ten months earlier, I was starting to feel comfortable in my new hometown.

But Lou and I were not getting more comfortable with our stepfather. And neither was our mother. She was betrayed by another of his lies: alcohol consumption. She was dead set against drinking alcohol and when they were dating my future stepfather had told her he did not drink. But he drank alcohol on their wedding day and on many days afterward. A few years later, I realized marrying my mother and taking financial responsibility for my brother and me was very likely a way for my stepfather to escape the Vietnam draft. He did tell one of his friends, after all, that he would rather "suck dick" than join the army, according to another family member. I also remember my stepfather saying he hoped being an elementary school teacher in a city where many young students lacked a good father figure in their lives could help him avoid the draft. In any case, if he had been honest with my mother about his taste for alcohol, she probably would never have married him. And he might have ended up in the army just like his younger brother, who was stationed in Vietnam during the late 1960s.

During the autumn of 1968 my stepfather joined a Friday night bowling league. After leaving the Broad & Bay bowling alley for the night he and his friends would go to a bar and drink. Sometimes he would come home smelling of alcohol and occasionally intoxicated. It typically led to fierce shouting matches between him and my mother that often spilled over to the next morning, even while our family went grocery shopping. Lou and I started doubting the marriage would last. We were beginning to think we would be fatherless again. But that prospect didn't frighten us as much as the intensity of the anger between the two of them. It was anger that we, along with our baby brother and eventually a sister, would be subjected to for several years.

In order to be in his good graces by acting "extra special nice" to him at the start of eighth grade, my stepfather wanted me to accompany him to Broad & Bay to watch him bowl in the Bloomfield Heights League every Friday night. It was a very boring outing for a young teenager that was only made tolerable by the presence of two other peers who would join me in the snack bar most of the evening. A few weeks into ninth grade, when my friends finally stopped coming to the bowling alley, I told my stepfather I wanted to collect payments from newspaper route customers on Friday nights instead of accompanying him to the bowling alley. He acted disappointed in me but finally stopped encouraging me to see him bowl.

He expressed some of the same expectations, and ultimately disappointment, after our family got our first color television. This happened right after we moved into our Birch Street house in the central part of Bloomfield, off of Broughton Avenue, during the autumn of 1969. My stepfather had favorite TV shows he insisted on watching, including *The Courtship of Eddie's Father*, *Room 222* and *Julia*. He wanted his family to watch these shows with him. So, I sat in the living room with him every week with waning interest. Finally, I joined my mother and Lou in finding excuses not to watch them with him. Again, he expressed his disappointment in me.

It was around this time, when I was thirteen years old, that my stepfather once hit me in anger. When he saw me raise my fists to defend myself, he backed up onto the couch and started kicking his feet at me.

During the fist and feet flurry that followed, one of his toes got broken. Lou recently reminded me how "pathetically comical" it was to watch him sigh for weeks afterward trying to make me feel guilty as he hobbled about with a cast.

As challenging as living in Bloomfield was for Lou and me those first years, we knew it was even more difficult for our mother. She was focused on satisfying the needs of her infant son and new husband in what was for her a new world. Her life had suddenly changed, and so did much of her enthusiasm for it, apparently. Lou and I realized we were no longer the most important figures in her life, as we had been just a year or two earlier. She had always been diligent about making sure we did our schoolwork when we lived in New York City, but she no longer mentioned it after we moved to Bloomfield. Even though we had little money, she had always made sure we had decent clothes to wear and good food to eat when we were younger in the city. After she married my stepfather, these no longer seemed to be priorities for her. My mother also used to find ways for our family to be able to enjoy amusement parks, sporting events, movies, festivals, parades, and other special events when we lived in New York City. When we moved to Bloomfield, we did little of this for a few years. She had liked to dance and listen to popular music just a few years earlier but seemed to have practically no interest in them a year after she married my stepfather.

The contrast between the kind of mother Elena had been before and shortly after she remarried was huge.

In late 1967, after over a dozen years of living in New York City where she had been able to walk to Spanish grocery stores, ride a bus or subway to visit her mother and brother, go to Spanish-language theaters and interact regularly with other Hispanics, my mother found herself in a completely different environment. While my stepfather worked a few miles away in Newark and Lou and I attended schools in Bloomfield, she stayed home during the day with my baby brother. She missed her mother, Abuela Belen—frequent toll calls were not in our household budget—and many of the things she had taken for granted in the city. I felt sad for her, although I did not express this because I was dealing with my own challenges adjusting to a new life in a new town with a stepfather.

The neighborhood in Bloomfield's Carteret School district was predominantly Italian American and there were no Spanish grocery stores or other evidence of Hispanic culture to be found within walking distance for my mother, who didn't drive at the time, although she was already bilingual. Her lack of access to Spanish food staples, along with a small household budget and lack of creativity in the kitchen were the main reasons family dinners became less appetizing to Lou and me. When Abuela Belen traveled by bus from New York City to visit us she usually brought with her a bag of black beans and a few other Spanish groceries. That ensured we would enjoy a few nice meals that week.

One day in 1968, anxious to step out of the house, my mother placed her youngest son in a baby carriage and walked to Milbank Park, which had a small playground. While there, to her surprise and delight, she heard a woman speaking Spanish with two young children. My mother approached the woman and a friendship that lasted the remaining forty-four years of her life was born.

It turned out my mother's new friend was a Venezuelan who lived with her husband and their two children across Bloomfield Avenue from Milbank Park. The two women would often meet at the playground, speaking their native tongue and finding comfort with a kindred spirit far away from their homes, figuratively, yet near their homes, literally.

Within a year after our family moved a few miles to the house on Birch Street in Bloomfield, an elderly Spanish couple began living in a house across the street from us. They were the first people from Spain I recall meeting. My mother became friends with them and even began occasionally babysitting their granddaughter, who was about the same age as my younger brother.

Many years later my mother became friends with a Cuban-born woman who began attending our church in Bloomfield. She once described her friend, an educated and professional middle-aged woman who also spoke with a strong Spanish accent, as "like a sister" she never had. My mother and stepfather became quite close to the Cuban woman and her second husband, a soft-spoken non-Cuban gentleman. They became like extended family to us. My mother was heartbroken when her Cuban friend and her husband decided to retire to Sarasota, Florida. In the spring of 2000, my wife and I and our young children had a wonderful visit with them at their Florida home.

Times have changed in Bloomfield since December 1967, when our family moved to the predominantly Italian neighborhood in the southern part of town. According to the 2010 census, a quarter of Bloomfield's approximately 47,000 inhabitants are Hispanic. Many of them live in the area between Grove Street and the Newark border in the Carteret School district where our family moved to shortly after my mother remarried. In 2013, a man named Joseph Lopez was elected councilman-at-large. Two blocks from the North 15th Street home where our family lived for almost two years, on First Avenue near the Bloomfield/Newark border, I noticed a restaurant called Havana Mia while driving through the neighborhood in 2020. I imagine my first years in Bloomfield would have been quite different—certainly I would have enjoyed dinners more—if there had been any kind of Hispanic presence around our home.

The Outcast in eighth grade

Chapter 7. The Younger Sibling: Brothers in Arms

Of all the people in this world, my big brother's life most closely resembles the journey of my identity. Like me, Lou was born in New York City, spent part of his pre-school years in Cuba, and lived much of his childhood in Manhattan before moving with our mother and stepfather to New Jersey. He started using our stepfather's last name the same time I did and together we tried to adapt to a new way of life. But Lou and I always looked different from each other. He was taller and thinner than me and began wearing eyeglasses many years before I did, which gave him a studious look. Whereas I physically resembled our father, my brother looked more like our mother. He inherited her overbite and was fitted with braces in his mouth to correct his "buck teeth" shortly after we moved to Bloomfield.

Another big difference with my big brother was that he and my stepfather never got along. My stepfather seemed to like me during most of our relationship because he thought I was fun to be with and I usually made him look good and feel proud. It was never the case with Lou, even though he was smarter and more courageous than I was. Lou didn't try hard or often enough to make our stepfather look good and feel proud. To his credit, Lou didn't want to make the relationship all about pleasing his stepfather. And our stepfather didn't try hard enough to understand my brother and make a serious attempt to bring out the best in him. Largely for this reason, Lou had a more difficult time living with our stepfather than I did between the time he was twelve and nineteen years old.

As soon as my mother married my stepfather, he became critical of the education Lou was receiving at his magnet middle school for gifted Catholic children, Msgr. William R. Kelly School. My brother had passed a tough exam in order to enroll in the school. It was something I was unable to do the following year after receiving no encouragement from my stepfather, a public-school teacher. Lou was thriving for over a year in the school before our family moved to New Jersey. He never thrived in school again.

He began attending a public junior high school when we moved to Bloomfield and seemed to immediately lose his motivation to excel in his studies. My brother didn't feel academically challenged and had the same difficulty making new friends as I did in our new environment. He had felt he belonged with his Kelly School classmates, but not his South Junior High School classmates. His grades quickly deteriorated. And so did his relationship with our stepfather, who became increasingly critical of Lou after we moved to Bloomfield. Rather than try to help my brother, our stepfather became more antagonistic towards him.

Lou remembers how our stepfather tried to make him feel guilty about the cost of his braces. He had promised to cover the cost since our family no longer qualified to have orthodontal work performed at no charge after the marriage, a situation that brought my mother to tears. Our stepfather accused him of being an ungrateful stepson and told our mother Lou was mentally and emotionally unstable. Eventually, Lou lashed out at our stepfather, pointing out he wasn't doing anything for his teeth that wasn't being done before. Preoccupied with her baby son and new life in New Jersey, my mother offered little defense for Lou, who years later said he felt we were "thrown under the bus" after she remarried.

Things got worse between our stepfather and Lou while we were in high school as my brother continued to underperform academically and distance himself from the rest of the family. For example, Lou didn't quite embrace the son and, eventually, daughter that our mother and stepfather had together. My brother did not apply to any colleges as he finished high school and continued working at a shoe store in Bloomfield after he graduated. He married his high school sweetheart, who also had a troubling situation at home, a year later. He changed jobs, went to college part-time, and eventually separated from his wife. In the summer of 1977, at twenty-two years of age, he decided to join the U.S. Army.

Just before I drove him to the station in Newark to begin his journey in the army, Lou went on a two-month cross-country trip. He hitch-hiked to California and back with nothing more than a backpack. He stayed with strangers who were willing to put him up overnight as he thumbed his way west and then back east.

When my brother returned to New Jersey, my mother and I were happy to see him safe and sound after his cross-country adventure. My step-father was seemingly not. After a few hours, he told Lou he was not welcome to spend the night at our house. Lou reminded my stepfather how strangers had put him up in their homes during his summer jour-ney. If he could not stay at their house that night, Lou promised they would never see or hear from him again. My mother spoke up on be-half of her son, both to Lou and our stepfather's surprise. My brother spent the night with us after all, but we didn't see much of him again afterward.

I can't blame Lou for starting a new life apart from his New Jersey fam-ily. Embarrassed for some unknown reason that his stepson joined the post-Vietnam U.S. Army, my stepfather never made Lou feel welcomed during his occasional visits. My mother was proud of her son's mili-tary service, on the other hand. She and I were grateful whenever he came to visit us after he finished his army assignments in South Korea and Louisiana. He then married a woman he had met camping in the Grand Canyon while hitchhiking cross-country. Eventually, he earned his undergraduate degree from Appalachian State College and then moved to Alabama. He settled in North Carolina after landing a teaching job in 1985.

A few months after his first son was born, Lou took a trip north to visit his mother, stepfather, me, my wife, and other family members. He decided to surprise our stepfather by showing up unannounced at the school where he taught, which was only a few blocks from the home my mother and he shared. But it was my brother who ended up surprised when the school staff told him his stepfather never told them he had a stepson who lived in North Carolina and now had a grandson as well. Knowing our stepfather well enough to imagine him bragging about his family, Lou was hurt that his stepfather had practically denied the existence of his eldest stepson and first grandchild. My brother pictured his stepfather talking instead about me and his two young children, who were well-known students at the school.

It was very interesting to observe the journey of my brother's identity during his new life with a new wife and family in Alabama and North Carolina. He became very close to his wife's family, admitting to me they made him feel like he was part of a family he never had growing up. In fact, he seemed to have little real interest in my mother and our stepfather's sides of the family as he and his wife raised their two sons in North Carolina. And he had no interest whatsoever in our biological father's side of the family for many, many years.

Lou's wife has a deep Southern accent, and over the years his voice began to also have a small touch of a Southern accent. Although he landed a teaching job in North Carolina that included Spanish instruction, Lou lost more of his first language skills than I did. By his own account, he was a hard-nosed teacher who seemed to have little patience for the very kind of high school student he himself had been. And unlike anyone we knew after our father and mother divorced, he became quite handy around his home and the rest of his property, taking on projects after researching them in a library before computers and the worldwide web were popular.

I was deeply touched by the strong and caring love my brother demonstrated for his second son, who was diagnosed with muscular dystrophy shortly after starting school and required a wheelchair by the time he was a teenager. Lou and his wife devoted their lives to giving their second son the best quality of life he could have while MD tried to do the opposite. The disease killed my nephew soon after he turned twenty-two years old, but Lou still loves the son he lost more than most fathers love the children of theirs who are still alive.

Our love for our sons aside, as we raised our families and eventually became empty nesters, Lou and I couldn't be more different. I'm a suburbanite who continues to draw energy from New York City. He's a Southern man most happy on the property he's overseen for over thirty years. Perhaps we always were different although we may not have realized it growing up with our divorced mother in the city and then our stepfather in New Jersey. But we've never grown apart over the years. We stayed close by writing often to each other, regularly talking on the phone, and occasionally traveling long distances to visit each other for days at a time. We've truly remained brothers in arms, with identities closer to that of anyone else in this world that were forged by the transforming experiences we shared.

The Younger Sibling and Lou in Havana (above) and Bloomfield (below)

Chapter 8. The Big Brother: Lovable Little Brother

Within a year of my mother's marriage to my stepfather in 1967, she gave birth to my baby brother, who I will refer to as Robert or "Rob" (not his real name). It was a joyous occasion for the family when he left Roosevelt Hospital a couple of blocks from our Amsterdam Houses neighborhood in New York City and came home to our apartment. Two months later, in December of 1967, our family moved to Bloomfield, where Rob lived for the next thirty-five years.

Technically, this blond-haired, blue-eyed boy was only my half-brother, of course. But I always regarded him (and the sister who followed a few years later) as a full sibling. I embraced this little half-Cuban, half-German American like a true brother. It helped that my mother was very fond and proud of her new son. I willingly changed his diapers and fed him when necessary and enjoyed playing and otherwise paying attention to him. Being eleven years older, I was almost like a third parent to him. I read to him, taught him how to throw and hit a little plastic ball and even walked with him to my barber for his first professional haircut. A while later, I would take him to Yankee Stadium once a year and we would sit with the "bleacher creatures" behind the right field wall to enjoy the games even more.

My little brother was a very mellow, agreeable, and lovable child. He smiled and laughed a lot and got along with everyone he met. He seemed to hardly change as he got older. Rob made new friends when our family moved from our Birch Street home to George Street in Bloomfield and he switched from Franklin School to Demarest School, where his father taught. The only time anyone remembers Rob being hit by his parents was after he tripped on stairs and accidentally dropped a cake he was carrying home from church one Sunday afternoon. In anger, my stepfather smacked Rob in the face and bloodied his nose. The incident horrified my sister, who was four years younger than her teenage brother.

Rob was athletically skilled enough to earn two varsity letters in baseball while at Bloomfield High School and played a lot of varsity baseball during his four years at Rutgers University-Newark. Rob was also an outstanding bowler, earning varsity letters in high school and competing in leagues as a young adult. In fact, he once bowled a perfect 300 in a sanctioned league game and has a ring from the United States Bowling Congress to prove it!

My mother credited Rob's hitting prowess to his Cuban genes. But she could never explain how his skill at hitting a baseball with a bat eluded his two older, full-blooded Cuban American siblings. My younger brother, according to my mother, ate more black beans than usual during baseball season and would request them the few times he was in a hitting slump. He was serious about his baseball and came to my wedding rehearsal with my stepfather with his uniform and spikes on after a game rather than leave early to be in the church on time with the rest of the wedding party.

Rob was clearly my mother's favorite child. Unlike Lou and me and our little sister, my younger brother never gave my mother any grief during the first twenty-two years or so of his life. That started to change within a few years after he graduated college when it became clear to my mother that her favorite son had acquired a taste for alcohol on weekends. His drinking disappointed her for a few years after he moved out of their home and into his own apartment less than a mile away, but she stood by him steadfastly. No one doubted Rob remained my mother's favorite child.

Rob clearly enjoyed his life as a bachelor for more than ten years after graduating college. An avid sports fan, he became enamored with Penn

State University football and for several years attended nearly all their home games in Beaver Stadium at University Park, Pennsylvania, with a childhood friend with whom he shared a pair of season tickets. The stories he told me about his autumn weekends in Happy Valley were quite entertaining, as were the stories I heard about him at the pub crawls in New York City organized by my wife's cousin and her husband, a Penn State graduate and Nittany Lions fan. My little brother will also admit he spent too much time at Fatso Fogarty's bar in North Arlington, New Jersey, around this time in his life. Although I'm certain he had many, I can only remember Rob introducing me to one girlfriend before he started showing up at family functions with a woman who he appeared to be in a serious relationship with in early 2000.

Although my mother never admitted it, it seemed to me she was ultimately heartbroken by my brother Rob's decision to get married. She had mixed feelings about his fiancée, but it's possible my mother would have found it difficult to embrace any woman Rob decided to marry. Still, she acted happy that he was finally going to get married at thirty-seven years old to a woman young enough to start a family with him.

On the morning of the wedding day, after she seemed fine at the rehearsal dinner the night before, my mother apparently became sick to her stomach and unable to get out of bed. She missed the entire ceremony and reception, lying in bed and supposedly frequenting the bathroom while her favorite son and the entire family celebrated just a few towns away. The next morning my mother seemed miraculously better. Perhaps it was a twenty-four-hour stomach virus—she was prone to them—that struck her on Rob's wedding day. Or perhaps the episode was psychosomatic, brought on by her internal conflict or stress.

It saddens me to see how my lovable little brother's life has played out since his marriage in 2005. At the toast during his wedding, I noted how happy he always seemed to be. Although our get-togethers and telephone conversations have become less frequent, I love him as much as ever. It is also heartbreaking to hear how negative his view of life has become. More than once, he has told me bad marriages are normal and good marriages are unusual. He believes most women change for the worse after their wedding and most husbands feel miserable and trapped by their marriage. My sister believes his definition of normal is largely based on the marriage of the parents he and she experienced growing up. Rob resigned himself to accept a role similar to our mother's, in an unhappy marriage he feels is actually normal.

My other siblings and I would never accept being in such a role. It's understandable that Lou and I have a different view of relationships than our younger brother considering the differences in our upbringing. But what is fascinating is how different my sister and younger brother's views are.

Chapter 9. The Proud Brother: Unsinkable Little Sister

I recall how proud my mother was of delivering her third and fourth children, twelve and nearly sixteen years after her first child was born. Her youngest child and only daughter, who I will refer to as Lauren (not her real name), was born while I was a sophomore in high school. My mother was beaming the day she left Mountainside Hospital in Montclair, New Jersey, in January 1972 holding my sister, a precious bundle of a baby who grew to physically resemble her father rather than our mother's side of the family with her blue eyes, blonde hair and tall, lean frame. I remember my classmates asking me for weeks, "Hey Charley, was that your mother who just had a baby?" "Yeah," I admitted, "that was my mom who just had a little girl."

From the moment she came home as the only child of my mother not born in New York City, my sister was different than my younger brother. She was full of energy, never napping as a baby! She would typically sleep through the night and then stay up for twelve or thirteen hours straight, which proved exhausting for my mother, who was in her mid-thirties. Also, unlike my mellow younger brother, my little sister was sassy. Lauren questioned many things, and if she didn't like an answer, she let you know. My stepfather, who I learned later on had been disappointed my sister wasn't a boy, found her quite a challenging child. My mother found raising Lauren nearly impossible and at times seemed to give up trying.

When my sister was nearly four, my mother needed to go back to work for a few months to help the family out financially. After we moved into a newly constructed house on George Street in Bloomfield before our home on Birch Street was sold, Abuela Belen stayed with us during the week to watch my sister. The two of them got along well. Belen, who had just retired as a seamstress, seemed to enjoy being with her spunky first granddaughter. She taught her a bunch of Spanish words and how to enjoy eating some Cuban food. After a few months, when our family's old home was finally sold, my mother resumed watching her young daughter full-time and Belen returned to her quiet life in New York City.

After only a couple of years in school it was apparent that my sister was quite a gifted child. Having learned to quickly read by herself, she was an exceptional student. She was also an outstanding athlete. When Lauren was only ten years old, my stepfather, his next-door neighbor (a German immigrant with two sons, one of whom was my sister's age) and I coached the co-ed recreation soccer team my sister played on. We could not believe how good she was. For the life of us, we could not figure out where she got her soccer talent. Although I was a big fan of the sport, no one in our family ever played it competitively. But there was Lauren, dribbling the ball past one boy after another, looking one way and passing blindly and accurately the other way, shooting rockets past goalkeepers. She was typically one of only two or three girls on the field and clearly the best player out there every game that autumn.

Lauren continued to excel in soccer as she got older, earning all-county honors when she played for Bloomfield High School. She also excelled in other sports, including softball, bowling and, before high school, field hockey and track and field. All the while, she remained an excellent student. She played varsity softball before graduating from the same Rutgers University-Newark campus her half-Cuban, half-German brother had. But unlike Rob, she passed the very difficult certified public accounting exam in one sitting. In 1998 Lauren was inducted into the Bloomfield High School Hall of Fame. Leading up to the induction dinner, my stepfather told her to make sure she gave him credit for her athletic accomplishments in her speech. Years later she told me it was typical of him to expect the glory of her accomplishments while she received little from them.

The truth is my sister was the least loved of my mother's four children. Sadly, my mother was older and physically and emotionally drained by the time Lauren was a teenager. My mother was constantly humiliated by my stepfather and felt trapped in another bad marriage. In hindsight, she probably also suffered from depression. She seemed to lack the energy and will to be the same kind of mother to my young sister that she had been to Lou and me when we were her age.

In 2012, moments after I delivered the eulogy at my mother's funeral in which I recounted the love I felt from her growing up and her other positive attributes, my sister whispered to me, "I wish I knew that mother."

My stepfather, who for years described Lauren as "difficult" to me, always acted as if his daughter wasn't nice or grateful enough to him to deserve his love. Clearly, he never seemed capable of loving his own children unconditionally. After looking up to her father like most children did, my sister felt "betrayed" by him before she was a teenager. From that point on, Lauren never pandered to him, unlike my brother Rob and me. Her accomplishments spoke for themselves. She refused to let her father treat her the same way he treated her brothers.

Tensions between my stepfather and sister continued to rise over the years despite her attempts to tolerate what she perceived as his selfishness. Knowing how much she loved her daughter, who was conceived with donor sperm through artificial insemination when Lauren was thirty-five years old with no potential husband in sight, she began thinking more about her own childhood and relationship with her parents. In 2015, seven years after she became a single mother, my sister decided to finally break off her relationship with her father. A few years later she told him she would welcome him back into her life on the condition that, in her words, "he tells and claims the truth, and is able to change, earn trust back and be able to be part of a healthy loving relationship."

"If he asked for forgiveness with the truth and changed, my arms are open to listen," Lauren told me in 2020.

As of 2021, no progress had been made in repairing their relationship. Lauren believes it is best for her young daughter and her not to be part of her father's life until such time that he can be truthful, feel remorse, and change into a trustworthy person. I understand and support her decision, and shortly afterward—during the middle of another family conflict—realized I also needed to break off communication with my stepfather.

It's been remarkable to see how much love my sister has for her daughter, who is my goddaughter, despite receiving such little love from her own parents while growing up. She understands how heartbreaking and difficult it is to grow up without feeling like your parents have your back and is determined to be the best, most loving mother she can be to her own daughter. Like almost everything else Lauren has tried to do in her life, she is succeeding as a parent.

To save face, it seems my stepfather has tried to convince some family members, close friends and even my sister herself (!) that I persuaded Lauren to cut off her father. He seeks to blame me for his only daughter and granddaughter having no contact with him. That is completely false, as my sister and me have ample evidence that he is an unabashed liar. The truth is Lauren did a lot of hard work analyzing her father and their relationship before getting to the point she is at today. If anything, it was the information and thoughts she shared with me during many long conversations that made me realize I was making the right decision to independently break off nearly all communication with my stepfather around the same time. I know he will never want to believe this or admit it to family and friends. He is apparently uninterested in truth and having genuine, positive, relationships.

Ever strong and courageous, my sister and her quarter-Cuban, quarter-German, and part Northern and Eastern European daughter moved from Wayne, New Jersey to the Asheville, North Carolina area to begin a new chapter in their lives during the summer of 2017. There is no doubt in my mind that when it came to bringing children into this world my mother saved the best for last. I am proud of my sister for everything she endured and overcame growing up in our family and keeping her faith in the plan God has for her. She is truly unsinkable.

The Proud Brother with siblings, 2014

Chapter 10. The Sportswriter: High School Years

It wasn't until I combined my passion for sports and writing and became one of Bloomfield's top young sportswriters during the early 1970s that I overcame the challenges of moving to a new town with a new stepfather three years earlier. It also erased some of the disappointment I felt in not being a good athlete, despite my strong interest in sports, particularly baseball. But it was also another reminder that I was different from my peers, few who seemed to like to write and even fewer who had any interest in journalism. I didn't fit in with the "jocks" who played sports in high school and proudly wore their varsity jackets. I certainly didn't fit in with the "cool" kids who wore long hair and fashionable clothes. Although I would have liked to look as stylish as many other students, my stepfather and our family's finances would not permit that. And I certainly didn't fit in with the academically gifted students in the National Honor Society, many of whom were part of other social cliques. I was ... well, I was simply "Charley the Sportswriter," with a mixed group of friends and acquaintances who came and went. My relationships with most of these friends had shallow roots and very few of them lasted beyond my high school years. I was reminded of this during the two high school reunions I attended. While many of my former classmates happily socialized with friends and acquaintances, I was largely by myself unless I approached them for some conversation.

By the time I was in my senior year of high school I was also, in the words of my two-year-old sister, "Charley Pimples." I had a mild case of acne during my sophomore year, and it remained manageable during my junior year, just like that of many of my peers. But by my senior year, the acne on my face was out of control. I tried all kinds of over-the-counter remedies to clear it up, but to no avail. Abuela Belen seemed to be the only one in the family who cared enough to try to help my condition. She would offer me advice when I saw her, but it still made little difference. Things finally changed when a woman across the street from our Birch Street house suggested I see the dermatologist where she worked. She pointed out that the office visits and prescribed medication would cost little or nothing since my stepfather was a teacher and probably had a good healthcare plan. Sure enough, over a half dozen visits to the dermatologist that summer where I got injections and pills cleared up my complexion by the time I started college in September.

I often blamed my acne for the relatively few dates and girlfriends I had during my teenage years. I became increasingly self-conscious around them as I turned sixteen and then seventeen and was often reluctant to strike up conversations or ask out girls I liked. I skipped my high school senior prom because I did not have a regular girlfriend or care to go with anyone else. While my classmates were posing for pictures with their tuxedos and gowns and, in many cases, riding to the prom in style, I was driving around town in a Volkswagen Beetle that evening delivering orders for Terry Drugs, the pharmacy on Broad Street in Bloomfield where I worked part-time.

When I look back, it was probably just as true that I simply did not know how to approach potential girlfriends or act around them. The Cuban stereotype of being suave and a good dancer did not apply to me or my older brother. Although I may have occasionally seemed confident on the outside, on the inside I was usually clueless about what I should be doing to make girls like me and want to go out with me. In a school as big as Bloomfield High, which had over 2,000 students in three grades when I graduated in 1974, I did manage to have a few girlfriends. We typically just hung out together around their home, occasionally going to a movie theater or some other place on a date. I should have been more considerate and fun to the girlfriends I had during my teenage years, who were all nice and kind. I just didn't know better until I was a little older and more mature. I don't think most boys at that time (and perhaps even today) had role models or others they could talk honestly with for advice about starting or maintaining relationships with girlfriends. And it took many more years and lessons for this Cuban American to learn how to dance!

There was a Cuban American teacher at Bloomfield High School who was the epitome of suave while I was a student. Mr. Gilberto Lopez (no relation) was probably no more than six or seven years older than me and was the sharpest dresser among the faculty, if not the entire school. He taught fine art, drove a new Datsun 260Z, and always moved with purpose, whether in his stylish platform shoes or Japanese sports car. I never took an art class in high school, but he supervised a study hall of mine. We made small talk (in English) whenever he slowed down or stood around near me long enough, and I learned he came from Matanzas in Cuba. He was the only faculty member who signed my yearbook with the words, "your friend."

When I was teenager, I hoped my proficiency in the Spanish language would improve by studying it in school. It didn't quite happen. I took a Spanish class while in ninth grade and got off to a great start with what I had retained by memory and speaking with Abuela Belen. That only got me so far, however. As the class progressed and studied more advanced words and grammar, I struggled to keep up. It was probably because of overconfidence and laziness on my part, but I also realized classroom Spanish was not the exact form of the language spoken by my Cuban family or Puerto Rican friends. I tried a bit harder to grasp the nuances of proper Castilian Spanish in class the following year but found it increasingly difficult even as I continued speaking basic Spanish with my abuela. My sister remembers that my stepfather did not encourage our mother to help us with our Spanish studies. I regret squandering the opportunity to improve my Spanish proficiency by not working harder at it during my high school years but came to under-stand that learning languages is easy for some people and more difficult for others. I am only half-kidding when I say I am still learning English, even after decades of writing in the language for a living.

There were only a handful of Cuban Americans and an equally small number of Puerto Ricans and other Hispanics at Bloomfield High School during the early 1970s. One of the Cuban Americans was a guy my older brother's age who had a sister that graduated with me and wrote in my yearbook, "As one Cuban to another, you're a real great kid." They were very nice, and we felt some kinship among us in a school of over 2,000 students, but we never got together after school or became close friends.

On the other hand, I became good friends with a Puerto Rican girl who was a sophomore in high school when I was a senior. Around the time I was graduating, I invited her to come with me and my family to our church's annual picnic at a lake about a half hour north of our town. When I told my stepfather I had asked a Puerto Rican girl to join us, he was clearly concerned and asked, "Is she a dark-skinned Puerto Rican?" I could not believe he asked such a question and replied she wasn't very dark. He was relieved and I was glad everyone treated her nicely at the picnic. We dated for several months, and I often enjoyed visiting with her at her family's house.

There was another Puerto Rican a grade ahead of me who was among the best athletes in the school. Because he starred for the school's foot-ball and basketball teams, I got to see him regularly in my role as a sportswriter. Sometimes we talked about foods we both liked. After he graduated, I lost track of him for forty-five years. We reconnected on *Facebook* and a year later saw each other at a multi-year Bloomfield High School reunion at a Jersey Shore restaurant near my home. He looked at me wearing my guayabera shirt and said, "Man, you look good." I smiled and returned the compliment.

During the summer between my junior and senior years in high school, I joined my family on a trip to Miami that I hoped would reconnect me with my Cuban roots. My stepfather, mother, abuela, little brother, sister, and I—that's six of us if you're counting—piled into a blue 1971 Dodge Coronet, our luggage in the trunk, for the long, scenic drive south. We stayed in cheap motels along the way and arrived in Miami Beach in the middle of a rainstorm. We rented two rooms in an art deco South Beach hotel, years before the resurgence of that part of town. My mother, Abuela Belen and I enjoyed reconnecting with some Cuban family and friends we had not seen in a while. I bought a white t-shirt emblazoned with the Cuban flag and the words, "I'm proud to be a Cuban." A huge disappointment, however, was that we did not eat at any of the many Cuban cafés or restaurants that were just a short drive away. My stepfather preferred dining establishments that offered a salad bar. So, we wound up regularly eating at mediocre spots with menus appealing to his taste buds and, apparently, those of many elderly Jewish people. We did not venture into Calle Ocho or other parts of the Little Havana neighborhood before returning home. But we did get to Disney World in Orlando, where I could swear I saw Cher at a restaurant with her then four-year-old daughter Chastity (now son Chaz). Oh well—at least I went to Miami and came home with a t-shirt.

Before leaving on that trip with my family, I worked a few evenings a week for almost two months at a doughnut shop and café on the corner of Broad and James streets in the North Center of Bloomfield. I didn't wait on patrons or take their orders. Quite the opposite. I cleaned up after them. In addition to the tables and floors, I had to clean the bathrooms. You can imagine the crap—literally—I had to deal with at that job. When I gave my two weeks' notice, I vowed never to take another job that required cleaning toilets. (And since then, I've never complained about cleaning the bathrooms in my own home.) I was glad to resume covering my high school's football and soccer games for the local newspapers that fall and very grateful when those seasons ended to land my part-time job at Terry Drugs, where my stepfather and a teacher friend of his also worked part-time.

The picture under my high school yearbook stated, "Charley enjoys working on and driving his 1955 Oldsmobile ... a permanent fixture at varsity games ... BHS top sportswriter plans to major in journalism and be a news writer." But I never drove a '55 Oldsmobile. The father of a friend of mine told me I could have the '55 Oldsmobile that sat idly in his backyard if I could get it to run. I bought a new battery for it, but lacking any automobile mechanic skills whatsoever, I never was able to get it to start.

For reasons I can't remember now, I had developed a fondness for old cars by that point in my life. A few months before I graduated, I had my eye on a 1958 Cadillac that was for sale a few blocks from my home. A cousin of my stepfather, a mechanic, took a look at it with me and discouraged me from buying it when he saw thick smoke coming out of its exhaust system. One of the earliest memories I have about maintaining cars involves that same mechanic. A few years earlier my stepfather drove his 1966 Ford Galaxie to the gas station where his cousin worked. When my stepfather complained about the problems he was having with the car, which had about 30,000 miles on its odometer by that time, his cousin opened the hood to take a look. He pulled out a dipstick from the engine and asked my stepfather when he had last changed the oil. "Change the oil?" my stepfather replied. "I didn't know I needed to do that." The mechanic grinned, and with that I learned my first car maintenance lesson.

Instead of a '55 Oldsmobile, I drove a 1965 Chevrolet Impala coupe during my senior year in high school, when the first gas shortage forced many drivers to wait on long lines at service stations. It had almost 100,000 miles on its smelly engine and was unreliable. Its gas gauge was broken and twice I ran out of gas while out on a date with a girlfriend. Once my stepfather's cousin came to my rescue and thought it was funny. Eventually my stepfather got rid of the Impala and bought a new blue 1974 Dodge Coronet. He let me drive the older (1971) Coronet sometimes for over a year and then asked me if I wanted to buy it from him. Knowing how he neglected caring for his cars, I declined the offer. Instead, I bought a 1970 Ford Thunderbird for about the same money the summer after my freshman year in college.

By the time I graduated high school, reporting on the various games that my Bloomfield High School classmates competed in gave me a sense of accomplishment, confidence and courage that had been missing. I stood up to the varsity baseball coach when he took exception to how I reported games for the local weekly newspaper. I responded to his scolding by saying my reporting was accurate and fair and challenged him to explain otherwise. A big, loud man nearing the end of his teaching and coaching career, he said I should just write what he wanted me to report, dismissing the idea it had to be truthful. I said I wouldn't do that and stopped reporting the baseball games. Two weeks later, the school's athletic director called me into his office and asked me to resume reporting the baseball games for the local newspaper. He agreed I should report what I thought was accurate and fair and apologized for the baseball coach's behavior.

I was glad I had stood my ground. Afterward, I never let a coach get away with berating me for a question I asked or story I wrote. Fortunately, most of the coaches I dealt with as a sportswriter, including George Cella at Bloomfield and later Bill Raftery at Seton Hall University, were gentlemen who understood I was a young sportswriter just trying to do a good job.

I was determined to be as good as some of the slightly older sportswriters in town and worked hard at it. I thrived on the recognition that sports writing gave me during my high school years. I also appreciated the support I received from the editors of the *Independent Press*, first Jean Hammond and then Russell Roemmele, who encouraged me to report about the school's athletic teams and trusted me with a few assignments around town that were not about sports. I was only paid $5 per article, which was well below minimum wage standards when the time I put into attending and writing about events is factored. But the knowledge, skills and experience I gained was enrichening. A couple of years after I graduated high school, I became the newspaper's first paid summer intern. Among the assignments I was asked to handle by Russell were obituaries. I will never forget how difficult it was to speak to a mother who had just lost her young son in an accident on a Jersey Shore amusement park ride.

When the Berlin Wall fell in autumn of 1989, Russell Roemmele published an article I wrote about my visit to the German city four years earlier on the front page of *Bloomfield Life*. Russell's work ethic, integrity and love for his family left a strong mark on me.

My work as a fledgling journalist during my high school years even made my stepfather proud of me, probably because he liked seeing his family name in the newspapers in such a positive way. After a short break as a college freshman to focus on my studies and working as many hours as possible at Terry Drugs to pay a portion of my tuition, I continued sports writing with much success through my college years.

The Sportswriter of Bloomfield H.S.

Chapter 11. The Card Shark: Flipping and Investing

Among my passions from the time I was nine years old in New York City and for almost twenty years afterward was collecting baseball cards. My brother and I began buying them in confectionery stores around the Amsterdam Houses neighborhood in the summer of 1965, when a pack of five Topps cards and a stick of bubble gum cost only a nickel. Because that was still a lot of money for us, we didn't exactly amass a collection that first year.

I got much more into baseball cards in 1966. By that summer, some of us collectors knew which store had the latest series of cards for sale and would walk several blocks to buy them there. I also started "flipping" cards, a form of gambling in which you would guess heads or tails and either win an opponent's card or lose yours to him depending on which side the card fell on the street after leaving your hand. I must have been pretty good or just plain lucky at it because I accumulated quite a few cards this way for a couple of years. I also started trading for cards I wanted from other collectors. Some kids (or their parents, perhaps) got tired of their old cards after a while and sold them cheaply or just gave them away to me.

By the time my family moved from New York City to Bloomfield after the 1967 season, I had amassed a collection of a few thousand baseball cards. Mets and Yankees players along with stars such as Willie Mays, Frank Robinson, and Roberto ("Bob" on at least one card) Clemente were my most treasured cards. I also had an affinity for cards of Cuban-born players. These included Pedro Ramos of the Yankees, and Tony (whose name was actually Pedro) Oliva, Zoilo Versalles, Camilio Pascual, Tony Perez, Cookie (Octavio, actually) Rojas, Bert Campaneris, Luis Tiant and a couple dozen other Major Leaguers. All these players had defected from Cuba or stayed in the U.S. after the Cuban Revolution when relations between the countries were severed.

According to the *Baseball Almanac*, over 200 Cuban-born players have appeared in the Major Leagues in the past 100 years. I was so proud when the Minnesota Twins had four of them on their 1965 American League championship team. Three of them were Black. Years later I learned that Black Cuban ballplayers were not typically embraced by either their Black American or white teammates. In a 2004 Ft. Lauderdale *Sun-Sentinel* article by Mike Berardino that was referenced in a study, "Left Out: Afro-Latinos, Black Baseball, and the Revision of Baseball's Racial History" by Adrian Burgos Jr., Tiant said about being excluded from the Black Aces club of twenty-game winners, "I haven't been treated like a white person here. In the minor leagues, I wasn't white. I was black. We couldn't eat in the hotel. We couldn't eat in the restaurants. And now I'm not black?"

Tiant's frustration is understandable. The ancestors of Black Cubans had more in common with Black Americans than they did with white Cubans, who were predominantly of Spanish descent, and other Latinos from the Americas, many of whom have indigenous ancestry.

In the early 16th century, the first ship containing African slaves arrived in Cuba to harvest the island's abundance of tobacco and sugar for export to Europe. By the middle of the 19th century, slaves comprised nearly a third of the island's population by some accounts. It wasn't until the 1880s that slavery was finally abolished in Cuba. Estimates of the Black population in Cuba today vary widely from under twenty-five percent to over fifty percent. But the percentage of Cuban Americans who are Black is probably just a fraction of that figure. According to a 1997 *New York Times* article about the small number of Black Cubans in the Miami area, "Black and Cuban-American: Bias in Two Worlds," the 1990 U.S. census figures show that, "Nationwide, black Hispanic residents were also 3 percent of all Hispanic residents."

According to the *Captivating History of Cuba* published in 2018, when Christopher Columbus "stumbled upon a land that struck him as spectacularly beautiful" on October 28, 1492, Taíno "Indians" were dominant in Cuba. But within twenty years, Spanish swords and diseases wiped out nearly the entire Taino population. Unlike in Mexico, Central America, parts of South America and other Caribbean Islands, there are virtually no Cubans or Cuban Americans of indigenous descent today.

In 1514, Cuba officially became a colony of Spain. Hundreds of thousands of Spaniards, perhaps millions, came to settle on the island during the next 400-plus years, even after Cuba gained its independence with the help of the U.S. around the turn of the 20th century. Nearly all white Cubans and Cuban Americans today have Spanish ancestry.

For the past several decades, perhaps longer, it seems white Cubans and Cuban Americans have been considered among the most "privileged" of Latinos in the United States. Personally, I've gotten that sense at times from fellow Latinos who learned I was Cuban American. I've also felt some resentment at times from other Latinos, mostly those who are Black or have indigenous ancestry. This is likely because of the history of Spaniards in the Caribbean Islands and Central and South America, and the discrimination Blacks and Latinos of indigenous descent continue to face in the U.S. today.

My mother and I saw old Black and white baseball players mix very amicably during the mid-1980s when we went to a Cuban old-timers event at the since-demolished Roosevelt Stadium on Kennedy Boulevard in Union City, New Jersey. The stadium was in the heart of the second biggest (after the Miami and Hialeah, Florida area) Cuban American neighborhood in the U.S. Few of the players whose baseball cards

I had collected were there. Most of the ballplayers were Cuban League veterans or ex-U.S. minor leaguers whose names I did not recognize. My mother and I were happy to be there, nonetheless. She got a particular kick out of watching the old-timers play and hearing another middle-aged woman say loudly, "¡*Qué buenos eran antes, pero qué viejo son ahora!*" ("How good they were once, but how old they are now!")

I continued buying baseball cards from candy stores in my Bloomfield neighborhoods for four years after I moved to New Jersey. In 1972, I started purchasing complete sets of Topps cards through the mail. I continued doing this for more than ten years and even ordered complete sets of cards issued by Fleer and Donruss after Topps lost their monopoly in the early 1980s. By that time, I had become more of an investor than a hobbyist. I didn't spend nearly as much time looking at and enjoying the cards. Card collecting had become an industry of sorts by the 1980s and I figured my collection might be valuable someday.

Lou also collected baseball cards when we lived in New York and first moved to New Jersey. He gave up the hobby for several years, then picked it up again during the 1980s. Of course, our mother never collected cards, but thankfully she never insisted we get rid of ours. Something the three of us did have in common was being smart with money. Lou and I weren't sheepish about working to earn it. And we generally didn't like wasting it. Heck, we didn't even mind saving a lot of it, which is something our stepfather also insisted on. In truth, we've had few financial issues in our lives since we finished college.

I once heard a half-Spanish half-Puerto Rican friend who was married to a Cuban American refer to Cubans as the "Jews of the Caribbean." A 2016 article in the *Jewish Chronicle* stated, "Cubans often describe themselves as the 'Jews of the Caribbean,' which is partially a reference to their large diaspora: two million live in the US." That may be true, but probably not the whole truth. I know my friend was equating the way she felt many Cubans seem to handle money with a Jewish stereotype.

Before they divorced, this Hispanic friend and her Cuban American husband met my wife and me at a Chinese Cuban restaurant in Union City for dinner. We ordered side dishes of fried rice and fried plantains to share with our main entrees. I will always remember how this restaurant, called La Gran China, was operated by three generations of a family whose members all had Asian facial features. The first generation included an elderly man who had been born in China and spoke a Chinese dialect. The second generation included his son or son-in-law, a middle-aged man who spoke fluent Spanish and proudly came to our table to show us a photo of him wearing a Cuban army uniform in his younger days. The third generation included a young man or teenager born in the U.S. who spoke perfect English with no accent. All three generations understood each other speaking in three different languages as they hustled around their crowded restaurant. You can't make this stuff up!

When my wife and I found ourselves financially stretched a year after the birth of our first son, sure enough, my baseball cards came to the rescue. I started looking at advertisements in baseball card hobby magazines for someone who might be interested in purchasing my collection. In one of them, I recognized a telephone phone number from a neighboring town. When I called, the man who answered expressed a strong interest in coming over to my home to see the cards I had for sale. A few evenings later, this short, fast-talking middle-aged man showed up at my door with a briefcase. His eyes lit up when he saw my mint-condition complete sets of cards from 1972 through the mid-1980s and some older cards of superstars. On the spot, he offered me a few thousand dollars for them. I agreed to part with them. He opened up his suitcase to give me the cash as I tried hard to contain my delight.

My wife and I couldn't believe our good fortune.

A few days afterward the man called back and raised his offer for my older sets of baseball cards. I agreed to part with most of them as well. He returned a couple of nights later with the same briefcase and gave me a few thousand more dollars as I handed over the cards I had bought from stores, gotten from trades with friends and won flipping as a kid. The man explained he already had buyers for these childhood mementos of mine.

But I did not part with my original 1965 Topps baseball cards. Because some of them were not in very good condition, I was only offered a few hundred dollars for this set of cards. I decided they were worth more to me for sentimental reasons and I've held on to them over the years.

My wife and I immediately paid off some lingering debt, paid cash to have a new roof installed on our house and bought our first compact disc player. I also got a bottle of premium Russian vodka to savor over the next few weeks. The baseball cards were clearly the best investments I ever made!

The Card Shark on the field

Chapter 12. The Lopez and Bruns: The Name Game

"Think about all the implications of changing a child's name before you go ahead. You need to be sure that such a big step like changing a child's name is the right thing to do in all the circumstances. Think about all who will be affected—the child, the father's feelings if the child stops using his name, and those of grandparents and other relatives. The child may resent it later in life and want to change their name back again. Building family togetherness does not depend on the use of the same family surname."

—from https://www.familylives.org.uk/advice/divorce-and-separation/your-children/how-to-change-your-child-s-surname/

Since my relationship with my stepfather was at times very difficult, why did I legally change my surname to his when I turned eighteen? That's a fair question I'm often asked. Truthfully, I had little choice. At the time, it seemed a "no-brainer."

I had been using the Bruns surname for over six years—the entire time I lived in Bloomfield—by that point. Except for my birth certificate and driver's license, there were few traces of my birth name left in my life by the time I legally became an adult.

When I started South Junior High School within a year after moving from New York my name appeared in class lists as "Charles (Lopez) Bruns." I told my teachers that I wanted to be referred to as simply "Charles Bruns" and explained it was the surname of my stepfather who I lived with. Some of them understood more quickly than others, but all of them obliged. The same thing happened the following year when our family moved to another home in Bloomfield, and I began attending eighth grade at North Junior High School. The next year and the following year when I began attending Bloomfield High School, no explanation was necessary. The Lopez reference had disappeared from class lists altogether. Teachers and everyone else in the schools simply knew me as Charles Bruns.

My older brother had a similar experience when he attended Bloomfield schools. Years later, he did share one particularly interesting exchange he had with a South Junior High School social studies teacher who was just about ready to retire. Stumbling over the dual references to Lopez and Bruns on his class list, the aging teacher asked Lou, "Lopez? Is that a Puerto Rican name?" No, it's a Cuban name, but you can refer to me as Bruns, my brother explained. The teacher paused a few moments, and then mumbled something about Lopez sounding like a Puerto Rican name.

For years, actually, some people aware of my birth name referred to me as a Puerto Rican. A few assumed I was of Mexican descent. And, of course, many invoked the name and accent of Ricky Ricardo of *I Love Lucy* fame when I told them I was of Cuban ancestry. Eventually, I started tiring of the Ricky Ricardo references and stopped finding them funny. I never found the humor in the Puerto Rican and Mexican references, which typically were intended to put me down. I often told the person using them that it simply made them sound ignorant.

The bylines of the newspaper articles I wrote starting in junior high school identified me as "Charley Bruns;" I preferred "ey" at the end of "Charley" rather than the more conventional "ie" (as in "Charlie") simply because it looked better in print.

Of course, the New Jersey Division of Motor Vehicles didn't care what I preferred to be called. If my birth certificate read, "Charles Anthony Lopez," then so would my driver's license unless I had other legal documentation to the contrary. This was true even twenty-seven years or so before the terrorist attacks of September 11, 2001, when identification became more difficult to prove and change for people in the state and around the country.

Lou blazed the trail for my legal change of name. After he turned eighteen in early 1973, he decided he would legally change his name to our stepfather's surname. He did it for pure and simple convenience, he says, since his bank account and other documents had the Bruns surname, and the Lopez name meant nothing to him at that point.

It cost my brother at least $400 to legally change his name, which was a significant amount for an eighteen-year-old earning $1.75 an hour. He did it with the help of our family lawyer and no financial assistance from our stepfather. Lou remembers our stepfather was not enthusiastic about him legally changing his name, which was odd since he was the one who had insisted we use his surname when the family moved to New Jersey in December of 1967. Because my brother was legally an adult by this time, there was no requirement that our stepfather "adopt" him in order to change his last name. The lawyer simply had to prove Lou had no criminal record, no debt he was trying to avoid paying, or other barrier to shedding his born name and using that of his stepfather. Within a couple of months, it was a done deal. Lou received an updated birth certificate from the City of New York with the Bruns surname and shortly afterward got a New Jersey driver's license with his new name.

It was the same for me. Shortly after I turned eighteen, I contacted the same lawyer and set the wheels in motion for my legal name change. I did not think long and hard about it. By that juncture in my life, my identity was "Charley Bruns," plain and simple. I was on the verge of graduating high school with a diploma that read "Charles Anthony Bruns" and I was enrolled at Seton Hall University to start my freshman year that fall with the same name. The paychecks I got from my part-time jobs working for local newspapers and being a deliveryman for Terry Drugs all were payable to "Charles Bruns." As was the case with Lou, it probably would have been more trouble to revert to using my legal name rather than my assumed name by that point.

So, with little serious thought, I legally changed my name when I turned eighteen in 1974, just as Lou had done a year earlier. In hindsight, I had little choice. If I did not legally change my name, I know my stepfather would have likely accused me of being ungrateful to him. I guess I was led to believe it was the right thing to do, just like my older brother had done. I thought this even though our stepfather never went through the trouble or expense of legally adopting us during the first six or seven years he and my mother were married. Adopting us in order to legally change our names before we turned eighteen likely would have required my biological father's consent and entailed a more complicated legal process along with greater expense for my stepfather. He did not assist me financially with the legal name change. Nor do I remember him expressing any pleasure or desire to celebrate when it was done.

For years, I would explain I had changed my name out of gratitude and respect for my stepfather since he had immediately assumed financial responsibility for my brother and me after marrying our mother in 1967. It's true he did not let this responsibility get in the way of attaining his goal of buying a house within two and a half years of getting married. And it's true that in practice his financial contribution was minimal. Lou and I did not eat or dress particularly well and we both began working part-time jobs as soon as possible in order to get some things for ourselves that many peers received from their parents. But it's also true our stepfather had assumed a responsibility shirked by our biological father, who rarely paid my mother for child support after they divorced. As troubled as our relationship was with our stepfather, we were grateful for his financial support. And if it ever seemed we were ungrateful to him, he reminded us time and again of what he was doing for us. If we did not continually express our gratitude with our words and actions, he acted hurt and then angry, accusing us of being ungrateful. Changing my last name to his, upon reflection years later, was simply another way I tried to please him. And it wasn't too difficult to do because I felt that I simply had little choice at that point.

Although I have not found any statistics on the percentage of people who take on their stepfather's name, I can bet it's a small number. I can't think of a single person (besides my brother) who ever told me he had done this. But, to repeat, it was not something I thought too much about when I turned eighteen because I had already been forced to use my stepfather's surname for almost seven years by the time I legally changed it.

Nearly forty years later, in 2016, a few months after my relationship with my stepfather had deteriorated to the point that we hardly spoke, I changed my *Facebook* identity from "Charles Bruns" to "Charles Lopez Bruns" with the following explanation:

"What's with the name? I was born Charles Lopez to Cuban immigrants in New York. After my mother remarried and our family moved to New Jersey, I began using the Charles Bruns name. Like other people who include their former last name on Facebook, I wish to incorporate my original surname in my Facebook identity. It represents a part of whom I've always been. That's all there is to it; nothing more, nothing less. I'm still the same Charley."

The post drew forty-nine likes, which is a lot for me, and eight comments. Someone who first met me when I began attending Carteret School after moving from New York City wrote, "Wow, I never knew that. I think you should as well!"

A cousin from my biological father's side of my family wrote, "Similar reasons as to why I added Lopez to mine too, although I ended up going through the official change as a middle name. I've been publishing with it for several years. Cultural visibility is important to me as well. All best to you, primo...."

My stepfather's brother wrote simply, "You are who you are." I liked that. I wish his brother also realized that. Unfortunately, as I had learned by that point, my stepfather was incapable of grasping the impact of his selfishness on others. He still needed those close to him to make their lives all about him.

The Lopez and Bruns brothers with Abuela Belen

PART 3: "Charles Bruns"

Chapter 13. The Pirate: College Years

As I approached my eighteenth birthday during my senior year at Bloomfield High School, another decision that wasn't very difficult to make was where to attend college. My first choice was Seton Hall University in South Orange, New Jersey, a private Catholic institution which was only about a half-hour drive from my family's Bloomfield home. It had an excellent communications program, and I knew two other Bloomfield High School graduates who became sportswriters after attending the university. I just needed to get accepted into Seton Hall and make sure I could afford the tuition. My high school guidance counselor, Mr. Richard MacNett, helped take care of the former. While I sat in his office, he called the university's admissions department to talk about my application. He explained that while my grades were only average, my extracurricular activities in the communication field were exceptional. After the phone call ended, he told me I would get accepted. Sure enough, I received an acceptance letter a few weeks later.

My stepfather and I reached an understanding about the tuition. We agreed to split the cost 50/50 after any scholarships and grants I received. My freshman year tuition was $3,000, which was a lot more than that of a state college like William Paterson. We both had agreed that Seton Hall was the best local college—going away to school was never an option we considered—because of its communication program. Half of the tuition was covered by scholarships and grants during my first two years at Seton Hall. We therefore each kicked in about $750 to cover the balance. Our family's income was too high to be eligible for grants during my last two years. As a result, we each had to pay more for me to finish. Still, I was grateful to graduate with little debt.

Succeeding as a student at Seton Hall University during the mid-1970s proved to be another way I overcame the difficult transition of moving from New York City to New Jersey. But even there, it was challenging for me to be identified as the Cuban American I am. I once attended a meeting of the Caribe club, an organization of Cuban students at the school. Although I didn't look any different than many of them, I sure sounded different. Unlike most of them, I had no trace of an accent and spoke poor Spanish. That and my non-Cuban last name, plus the fact I had been born in the U.S. rather than Cuba, probably prevented them from quickly making me feel welcome in their club. I also sensed I didn't belong in the club and never attended another meeting.

Undeterred, I placed a small sticker of the Cuban flag on the rear bumper of my 1970 Ford Thunderbird during my sophomore year. It was the only Cuban symbol I noticed on campus during the four years I spent at Seton Hall. Hopefully, none of the few other Cuban Americans on campus who noticed it didn't interpret the bumper sticker as showing my support for Fidel Castro's Cuban government!

The majority of the liberal arts students I knew at Seton Hall during the mid-1970s were politically liberal, which was different than my political views. Already aware of the horrors of the Communist political and economic system in Cuba, and also influenced by the political views of my stepfather's family, I was a conservative Republican as a young adult. Even in the post-Watergate era where being a liberal Democrat was clearly fashionable on college campuses, I expressed my different political views to friends who were interested. Some blew me off as ignorant. Fortunately, others respected my viewpoints or at least my right to feel the way I did given my Cuban ancestry. (Maybe I should have discussed politics at the Caribe club meeting!) But it did make me feel different and an outsider and seem a bit "uncool" during my college years.

A cool thing I did do while I was at Seton Hall was learn to be a good photographer. It's a skill that has served me very well through life as a chronicler of family and friends, special moments, and interesting sights. Whether it's an event, vacation, business trip or simply a day in a city or countryside, I've almost always been there with a camera. My wife and two sons are major beneficiaries of what I learned while at Seton Hall, with many photo albums full of memories.

I bought my first camera, a bulky 35mm single lens reflex (SLR) model assembled in East Germany, in a midtown Manhattan store for less than half of the price of popular Japanese SLRs early in my sophomore year. The friend who recommended the Hanimex Praktica Super TL camera joined me for the purchase. Afterward, we drove to the Cloisters Museum in Fort Tryon Park in Washington Heights, Manhattan, near the George Washington Bridge, to test it out.

This friend was the same person who, a year earlier during our freshman year, debated me about whether Cubans were better off under a Communist government than they had been before Fidel Castro took power. She believed Cubans were better off under Castro. I argued they were not. The debate grew heated, and at one point our professor told me to calm down. Despite our major difference of opinion, she and I have remained friends to this day. When it was announced forty years later that the U.S. and Cuban governments were taking steps to normalize relations, she was one of my first friends to reach out to me about my feelings. I responded to her and others with the following sentiments on my blog, *1400 Characters*:

"I have positive, albeit mixed, feelings about today's announcement.

"The Castros have a lot of blood and theft on their hands. Their oppression of countrymen during the past 55 years is unforgivable. Ultimately, however, it is the Cuban people who will benefit from normalization of relations with the U.S.—as will the American people.

"As long as today's announcement will not exonerate the Castros—history should place them along Stalin, Hitler and other tyrants—I agree the time has come for a change. While I sympathize with Cuban Americans who lost loved ones to firing squads or knew of people who rotted in jails for daring to speak out for values that Americans take for granted, or had what was rightfully theirs confiscated by a one-party government, I laud President Obama for making the courageous decision to put the welfare of everyday Cubans above politics.

"It is these everyday Cubans, most of whom have never lived under a leader not named Castro, that we should think of and hope for today."

My photography teacher at Seton Hall, Jim Cummins, was a professional photographer who emphasized how to compose a frame, set the right exposure, and time a shot. He explained why the ASA/ISO setting, f-stop, and shutter speed matter. I always remember how he emphasized technique over equipment, making me understand that a skilled photographer can more easily take a great picture with a cheap camera than an unskilled photographer can with an expensive camera. I reconnected with this adjunct professor forty years later. He remembered our class and was pleased I reached out to him. I wrote on my blog that he never said anything about "the famous people he captured on film during his career. He knew the class was for the benefit of his students, not his ego. It wasn't until many years later that I learned he had photographed Jimi Hendrix, Janis Joplin and many other stars and garnered numerous accolades for his great work."

Seven years after I graduated from college, I applied some of the photography skills I learned from my professor to become "Charley the Wedding Photographer." After watching me take some pictures at the wedding of my brother-in-law and his new wife, the photographer from a popular studio in the North Center of Bloomfield asked if I would be interested in working with his studio. I said yes, and subsequently assisted him at a few weddings before taking on assignments for his studio later that spring and summer. I learned much about posing individuals and composing group shots. But lugging two medium-format cameras and heavy battery packs and film supplies that required constant monitoring and changing was challenging. It was difficult dealing with brides who wanted me to take great pictures while being invisible, bridegrooms who typically didn't want to bother posing for pictures, and drunk uncles and cousins who insisted I photograph them with long-lost family members. Those weekend assignments proved much more stressful than my regular full-time job, and by that autumn I told the studio head I had enough and quit. But the photography skills I acquired in those months were a great complement to what I learned in college.

Seton Hall was also where, just before I turned twenty, I finally learned to speak English with almost no trace of an accent. I began speaking English during my first few months after returning to New York City from Cuba when I was six years old. Of course, after speaking Spanish during the first six years of my life, I started speaking English with a Spanish accent. Although the accent slowly but surely began to fade during my early years at Saint Paul the Apostle School, someone told me when I first moved to New Jersey while in sixth grade that she detected an accent. I believe she was referring to some kind of Spanish/New York City mix in my voice by that time. My Spanish accent disappeared rather quickly while I lived in New Jersey but apparently my New York City accent, as evidenced by the way I pronounced words like "chocolate" and "coffee," did not.

When it came time to give my first speech during an oral communication class in my sophomore year at college, my professor, Joseph Peluso, stopped me numerous times to correct my pronunciation. Thinking I had no trace of an accent left in my voice, I was startled by all the errors in my speech he pointed out. He said it was clear to him I had lived in

New York City and would have to try harder to eliminate my regional dialect to be an effective communicator. Since I was a communication major, I agreed that would be a good idea. I worked hard during the rest of my time at Seton Hall and early years as a communication professional to speak without a New York City dialect. I want to believe I have succeeded, although people in other parts of the U.S. sometimes claim they can tell I am from the New York City/New Jersey area.

Other areas of study I particularly enjoyed during my time at Seton Hall were classical Greek dramas and novels by D.H. Lawrence. Over two classes with light enrollments taught by Father Eugene Cotter, I read all the surviving dramas by Aeschylus, Sophocles, and Euripides. I was fascinated by these ancient tragedies. Ten years later, I wrote a drama in the classical Greek style, complete with a chorus, about the U.S. air strikes in Libya. I was even more enthralled, however, by the early 20th century novels of D.H. Lawrence after reading *Sons and Lovers* in an English literature class taught by Dr. Rose Gallo. She encouraged me to read his other novels, which I continued doing after graduating college, and she was happy to receive the letter I wrote to her after visiting Lawrence's hometown of Eastwood, Nottinghamshire, in England during 1985.

I also developed a passion for the words and music of Bob Dylan during my years at Seton Hall. Just as the spring semester of my freshman year began, Dylan released his masterpiece album, *Blood on the Tracks*. I had heard some of his previous recordings over the years on the radio and during visits to New York with Abuela Belen and Uncle John, who had Dylan's *New Morning* album and his songs from *The Concert for Bangladesh*. But the ten songs on *Blood on the Tracks* blew me away. By the end of the semester, I bought a handful of old Dylan albums. That fall, I drove my 1970 Thunderbird a few hours to Hartford, Connecticut with some college friends to see him perform in concert with the Rolling Thunder Revue. I've seen Dylan in concert eighteen other times since 1975 and appreciated all his albums during the past forty-five years. Perhaps I'm among his biggest Cuban American fans. I believe that unlike the Rolling Stones, who I saw in concert at Madison Square Garden with my brother Lou at the end of my freshman year, Dylan has never performed in Cuba.

While taking a short break from sports writing during my first year at Seton Hall, I fancied myself a potential music critic. The problem was I didn't really know much about music or critical writing. When I approached an editor for the school newspaper, the *Setonian*, he suggested I draft a review of the new Loggins and Messina album. I proceeded to buy the album at a local record shop, listen to it a few times, and write a song-by-song critique. It must have read like an album review written by a sportswriter because the editor never published it. But two years later, after learning a lot more about music and critical writing, the *Setonian* did publish my review of the new David Bowie album.

I resumed sports writing during my sophomore year, but not for the school newspaper. I went straight to working for a local daily newspaper, a job many communication majors at the school who were aspiring journalists would have liked to have. I did, though, agree to contribute an article about the school's baseball team to my graduating class yearbook.

A couple of times while I was attending Seton Hall, the daily local newspaper I worked part-time at assigned me to cover the school's basketball game at Walsh Gymnasium. Talk about a "conflict of interest!" I was already a big fan of the Seton Hall Pirates basketball team, having first seen them at Walsh Gymnasium while in high school after a Bloomfield star had gone on to play for them. I attended a few games on the Seton Hall campus each winter while I was a student. So being asked to cover their games for a local newspaper was a dream assignment for me.

I've been a Seton Hall basketball fan for the rest of my life. For three years after graduating, I had a pair of season tickets and attended all their games with my girlfriend. She became my fiancée and then my wife during the initial seasons of the Big East Conference. We sat next to a fellow Seton Hall graduate and friend of mine who was the best man at my wedding, and a woman who also became his wife during those years. I've attended many Seton Hall games with my college friend as well as my wife and two sons over the ensuing years.

I would have attended more Seton Hall basketball games and participated in additional school activities on campus as an undergraduate student, but I didn't live on campus. Seton Hall was predominantly a commuter school at that time, and I was among the approximately seventy percent of the students who drove to the school to attend classes. Going away to college was never an option for me. My stepfather commuted to a local state college from his Bloomfield home in the early- to mid-1960s, and it was understood I would do the same after graduating Bloomfield High School.

My stepfather allowed me to occasionally drive the family's second car, a 1971 Dodge Coronet, from our Bloomfield home to the South Orange campus during my freshman year. On other days, I would get a ride from Bloomfield kids I knew who also commuted to the campus. During my sophomore year, I commuted to school in a 1970 Ford Thunderbird I purchased from the boyfriend of a woman I worked with at Terry Drugs. It was a big and great looking coupe, but it was in constant need of tune-ups and repairs while averaging under ten miles to a gallon of gas. I liked Thunderbird cars a lot, nevertheless, and was quite proud to drive it.

During the summer between my sophomore and junior years at Seton Hall, an elderly Terry Drugs customer who I regularly delivered prescriptions to remembered how much I liked her 1965 Ford Thunderbird. She asked if I wanted to buy it. When I asked her the price, she replied, "Three hundred dollars." Grateful she would sell me such a nice car for that price, I returned the next day with the cash and a cake from the bakery. The 1965 Thunderbird proved more reliable than the 1970 Thunderbird I sold to a friend. But unfortunately for him, the transmission failed within a month. I also had the misfortune of having my 1965 T-Bird smashed a few months later by a young woman who drove her car through a stop sign. It was barely drivable afterward. Eventually, my insurance company declared it a total wreck and paid me more than my purchase price to junk it.

I bought an early '70s Triumph Spitfire convertible during the summer before my senior year. I did not know how to drive a manual transmission car, but I figured it out while driving home from an auto parts store where the seller worked.

When my mother first saw the little two-seat convertible when I arrived home, she was astonished and asked, "Charley, is that a real car?"

"I hope so, Mom," I replied. "I paid real money for it." Shortly afterward I took her for a ride in it. She then realized it was both a toy and a real car. An expensive toy for her son, it turned out.

I quickly learned not only how to drive a five-speed stick shift, but also why the previous owner worked in an auto parts store. During the ten months I owned the Spitfire, the savings in my bank account dwindled from over $1,000 to under $200, even while I paid for some repairs with money I earned from working two part-time jobs. Primarily because of the car's impact on my finances, I backed out of a spring vacation trip to Fort Lauderdale, Florida, with some of my college friends. But I never forgot how to drive a manual transmission car and bought two others later in my life, including a Pontiac Fiero before I turned thirty and a Scion tC as I approached my fiftieth birthday.

I remember driving my Spitfire to Mother's night club on Route 23 in Wayne, New Jersey shortly before starting my senior year to see an exciting rock 'n' roll band, Wowii, play on Thursday nights. I was impressed with the quality of their covers as well as their original songs. What I thought was especially cool about the band, though, was that it was mostly comprised of Cuban Americans from Miami. There was nothing Cuban about their "power pop" sound, but I occasionally spoke to one of the five-piece band's members off-stage about Cuban food, which he missed eating.

By the time I graduated from the Catholic university in New Jersey that is Seton Hall, I realized the two paths in my life—one being the original path of the Catholic New York boy, the other being the subsequent path of the New Jersey teenager—had converged. I was "back on track," and felt great about it. When I finished college, I knew I had arrived at the station in my life that I had been destined for all along. I felt I was well on my way to leading the kind of quality life that my parents originally envisioned for their children when they had emigrated from Cuba, even though they were unable to economically advance their lives before getting divorced.

The Pirate at Seton Hall U.

Chapter 14. The Young Star and Old Guy: A Long Career

My career as a communication professional began as a journalist—a sportswriter, to be precise. When I was in ninth grade, I began writing and duplicating on a mimeograph machine a single sheet newsletter with National Hockey League standings and news. Initially, the newsletter was done as a school club project and distributed to a dozen teachers in the North Junior High School faculty lunchroom where I worked as a cashier. Within weeks, I had expanded the newsletter to two pages and began sharing it with many classmates.

That same winter, I began attending basketball games at the junior high school and writing bylined short articles about them for the weekly Bloomfield newspaper, the *Independent Press*. I also reported on the baseball team in the spring. When I began my sophomore year at Bloomfield High School, being the low man on the sports reporting totem pole around town at the time, I could only write about the football and basketball teams for the school newspaper, the *Student Prints*. That spring, I also wrote about the school's track and field team for the town and school newspaper. The following school year, I was the sports editor for the school newspaper, wrote bylined articles about the school's football, basketball, and baseball games for the *Independent Press*, and called in the results of the games to the local daily newspapers, the *Star-Ledger* and *Herald-News*, for extra cash. During the fall of my senior year, I was at the right place at the right time reporting about the school's outstanding football team for interested sports fans in Bloomfield and the surrounding area. To expand my sports reporting knowledge and experience, I also chose to write about wrestling that winter. The *Independent Press* editor took me under his wing and began challenging me to also report about non-sports events around town, which I gladly did.

So, it was no surprise that while I attended Bloomfield High School I was known as "Charley the Sportswriter." My career in the newspaper business actually began a few years earlier when I was known around the neighborhood, along with my older brother, as "the paper boy." I began delivering *Independent News* newspapers every Thursday after school in September 1969. I earned cash to buy baseball cards, magazines, records, snacks and also save money for other items I would want in the future. These included things most children seemed to get from their parents, e.g., clothes. The following September, Lou and I began delivering *Star-Ledger* newspapers every morning. In the spring of 1971, the rival *Evening News* went on strike and then ceased publication altogether after a short-lived return in the summer of 1972. By that time, our *Star-Ledger* routes had doubled in volume. We were making such good money that our manager was compelled to reduce the geographical area of our routes.

My experience delivering newspapers, which eventually overlapped with the beginning of my career as a sports reporter, was largely positive. One of the worst parts about it, though, was a bizarre rule our stepfather established about our daily deliveries. Once we went outside to check if the newspapers had arrived, we had to stay outside. He would not allow Lou and me to come back inside the house after we stepped outside if our newspapers had not yet arrived. He made this rule so the sound of the doors wouldn't disturb his sleep. If the newspapers were late, we were stuck outside by our stepfather's rule. Sometimes we passed the time by walking a few blocks to a bakery or confectionery store for glazed donuts or crumb buns. But usually we waited inside our garage, which of course was not climate controlled. We waited until the newspapers arrived or an hour had passed, when we knew our stepfather had awakened.

My career in the newspaper field as a sportswriter got a major boost in January 1976, when I was a sophomore at Seton Hall University.

A fellow Bloomfield High alumnus and recent Seton Hall graduate I knew asked if I was interested in a part-time position at the *Herald-News*, where he worked as a full-time sportswriter. The job had opened because another Bloomfield High alumnus and soon-to-be Seton Hall graduate left the *Herald-News* to pursue what turned out to be an outstanding broadcasting career, eventually landing at ESPN and earning multiple Emmy Sports Awards. Although I had been taking a break from sports writing since starting college in order to concentrate on my studies and make some decent money delivering for Terry Drugs, I said yes without hesitation. I interviewed for the job at the newspaper's Passaic, New Jersey office, and accepted an offer to start almost immediately that winter.

My boss, Bruce Keenan, who was only in his mid-thirties at the time but looked fifteen to twenty years older, was among the most interesting individuals I met at the *Herald-News*. I still remember the first words from this Vietnam veteran and alcoholic when I walked into the office and introduced myself. "Sit down," he said, a toothpick in his mouth and a yardstick protruding from the back of his shirt so that it was handy when he laid out stories in the sports section. After he found out I was a Cuban American, he often referred to me as a "wetback." Despite this, Bruce and I got along just fine most of the time. Working with him reinforced in me there are lessons about life, good and bad, that can't necessarily be learned from written or spoken words but, rather, by simple observation and reflection.

Perhaps the reason he told me to sit down when we first met was so that I could be a good observer, which is an important skill for a journalist, after all.

I enjoyed sports writing at the *Herald-News* and, in particular, the company of nearly all of the other sportswriters on the staff. Typically, four or five of us sat by each other in an open office answering phone calls from correspondents who were reporting the details of high school basketball, baseball, or football games. We then would write a couple of paragraphs and assemble a box score on each of the games.

Just a couple of years earlier, I had been the student calling local daily newspapers with the results of my high school's game. Now I was on the other end of the line, taking the information and writing what was published in the next day's edition of the *Herald-News*. But it was just as much fun to talk sports in between the calls with the other writers whose names I was already familiar with from reading their stories over the years.

A few times during basketball and baseball seasons and every Saturday during football season, I was assigned a game to attend and write a full article about it when I returned to the office. These kinds of assignments were my favorite. I would take detailed notes at the game, talk to the coaches afterward, and then think about the lead and angle for my story while driving to the *Herald-News* office on Main Street near the Passaic-Clifton border. As soon as I arrived, I would write my story. Sometimes Bruce would wait patiently for me to finish my article so that he could "wrap up" the sports section and leave.

My most memorable assignment at the *Herald-News* was the 1977 U.S. Open tennis tournament men's final. In the last U.S. Open held at the West Side Tennis Club in Forest Hills, Queens, an Argentine, Guillermo Vilas, came from behind to beat defending champion Jimmy Connors in four sets. After the match ended, Vilas spoke to reporters in both English and Spanish. I was able to understand what he said to Spanish-language reporters and was pleased to use the information in my *Herald-News* story.

During my two-and-a-half years there, the newspaper business began its transformation to the computer age. When I first started, I wrote all my stories on an electric typewriter. That was already a step up from the manual typewriter I had used to write newspaper articles while in high school. My *Herald-News* boss edited the drafts, and unless some text needed to be rewritten, he walked to a room in the back of the building where the stories were typeset before being printed. Within two years, new terminals replaced the typewriters on our desks, and I was writing stories on "VDTs" (video display terminals). These terminals were a bit unreliable, unfortunately, and occasionally would "eat" stories before they were edited or forwarded to the back office. More than once, including Thanksgiving Day 1977, I needed to rewrite my story—a frustrating and difficult task at times—while a deadline loomed, and my boss patiently waited.

With years of experience for such a young sportswriter and a real commitment to making every story I wrote a minor masterpiece, my *Herald-News* bosses recognized my good work. As I prepared to graduate Seton Hall, the newspaper offered me a full-time position. I turned it down. A few weeks later, Bruce and the other sportswriters joined me at CBGB, the New York City music club at the height of its fame, for a farewell celebration. Bruce and I and one other sportswriter had a fun time seeing Debbie Harry of Blondie and others perform at a benefit show that evening, even though we were out of place among the punk rock fans. All the other writers were unfamiliar with Debbie Harry, uncomfortable with the scene and couldn't leave the Bowery club soon enough.

Rather than continuing to work at the newspaper, I had decided to accept a full-time public relations and internal communication position with Research-Cottrell, a pollution control equipment manufacturer where I had also worked part-time during my senior year. That's right, while a full-time college student earning an undergraduate degree in communication, I held two part-time jobs in the communication field. By working long hours and not always having time to eat three meals a day, in less than a year I lost the thirty pounds I had gained since starting college. I was back to my high school graduation weight by the time I finished college.

Why did I abandon my passion for sports writing by the time I was twenty-two? Primarily because the corporate job paid better and offered regular hours, which was a major disadvantage at the newspaper where working days and hours varied week-to-week. This made it difficult to plan social and other non-working activities. Consequently, "Charley the Sportswriter" became "Charley the PR Man."

I began working full-time at the Bedminster, New Jersey headquarters of the pollution control equipment company right after graduating Seton Hall in May 1978. I wrote and edited the company's employee newsletter and took on some other writing assignments and communication projects. As part of Research-Cottrell's corporate communication team, I helped put the company's annual report "to bed" at a printing press in lower Manhattan, a milestone which we celebrated with a dinner at an upscale Italian restaurant in Little Italy that same evening.

My department was headed by a relative of a pharmacist I knew at Terry Drugs in Bloomfield by the same name. This executive was a cigar-smoking, stylishly dressed, no-nonsense guy and a former sportswriter himself. I would get a big kick out of seeing him go out to lunch sometimes with the company's chief executive officer. This CEO, whose shiny black Cadillac Fleetwood stood out in the parking lot, would need to squeeze his six-foot-plus frame inside my department head's small, non-descript fifteen-year-old General Motors sedan with faded paint. "You never want a boss to think you might be making too much money," he said about the car he drove a few miles to work. Meanwhile, he left the newer family car at home with his wife. It was not a belief shared by my stepfather, who for about the last fifteen years of his teaching career would drive his late model full-size Cadillac or Lincoln sedan half of a mile and park it in his school's lot.

The ups and downs of my corporate communication career began almost immediately when I lost my full-time public relations and internal communication position after a few months. A financial downturn at the pollution control equipment company led to layoffs. I reported a few high school football games for the *Herald-News* that fall while looking for a new full-time position. Once more the newspaper offered me full-time work. And once again I turned them down, this time to accept a communication position with Vibra Screw. This small family-owned industrial equipment manufacturer in Totowa, New Jersey offered me a significantly higher salary than the *Herald-News* did, along with free nights and weekends.

I learned corporate communication work inside out during the nearly three years I spent at Vibra Screw. Even though I was just twenty-two and less than a year out of college when I began working for them, the company's executives recognized my strong work ethic right away and immediately gained confidence in my ability to quickly learn how to get things done right. It helped a lot that my predecessor at the company was a veteran advertising man who decided to retire but remain available as a consultant. He became my mentor, particularly in writing promotional copy. It's quite different than writing newspaper copy.

While at the company, I made my first business trip, to a coal mine near Tulsa, Oklahoma, where I supervised the photography for a new advertisement. Since I was too young to rent a car, I relied on taxi cabs and a Vibra Screw sales agent to shuttle me around. A year later, I went on my first overseas business trip. I accompanied two salesmen to a trade exhibition in Birmingham, England, for a week that opened my eyes to international business and a completely different way of speaking English.

A lasting memory of my time at Vibra Screw was the weekend in April of 1979 when the company hosted a national sales meeting as it approached its 25th anniversary. The family that owned the business spared no expense in making sure its sales agents and employees enjoyed the occasion. My girlfriend and I enjoyed a Broadway show and being at The Grand Ballroom at The Plaza for a banquet that was among the most elegant I've ever attended in my life. This landmark hotel on Central Park South is less than a mile from the Amsterdam Houses neighborhood where I lived as a child, but it may as well have been in a different world. Such are the fascinating contrasts of New York City and the world we live in.

One of my co-workers at Vibra Screw was a Cuban immigrant just a few years older than me. Like many Cubans in New Jersey at the time he lived in Hudson County and married another Cuban during the three years we worked together. I was impressed by how well he played basketball during our lunchtime games, and also at how he turned a deaf ear to being called "Fidel" by an older man who worked at the same company. He did a better job than I did ignoring that wise ass.

I sometimes wonder how different my life would have turned out if I had decided to pursue my passion for sports writing full-time rather than launch my corporate communication career after college. Perhaps I might have had more fun, memorable moments, and some fame as a sportswriter, as many in the talented bunch of young guys I worked with at the *Herald-News* did as their careers unfolded. I'm certain, though, I earned more money and have led a more stable and fulfilling family life with the career path I chose. I have no regrets with the direction I took my career, despite the twisting journey of my career as a PR man.

It's interesting to reflect on the impact my identity and "misleading" surname had on my career. It's possible some of my employers during the 1970s and '80s might have been reluctant to hire a man named Lopez for a job that required strong writing and other communication skills, such were—are?—the stereotypes of Latin Americans' proficiency in English. I'm certain the Bruns surname did me no harm when I sought to move to a bigger company and landed a corporate communication position with Siemens, a Germany-based electronics and electrical engineering conglomerate in 1981.

I made many friends during the eight years I spent at Siemens, where I often was made to feel like a young star. My first supervisor there, in fact, once gave me as a gift a piece of artwork depicting a "young star." My boss during most of those years was a deep-voiced man who counted on me time and again to help generate more work for our advertising and design department. I essentially functioned as an account executive for our in-house agency, pitching clients and then developing strategic marketing communication plans and managing print advertising, direct mail, and promotional brochures projects for them.

I generated a five-fold increase in billings during my six years as an account executive for the Siemens in-house agency, much of it in competition with external agencies. The company valued my contributions enough to gladly take me back when I left them for a month in 1983 to join a company outside of Boston for a position I quickly regretted. I didn't skip a beat when I rejoined Siemens.

My clients included the company's graphic arts production, telecommunication switching, cardiac pacemaker, respiratory therapy, hearing instruments, health physics, medical ultrasound, nuclear medicine, and security businesses. Most of my clients were in the New Jersey and New York area, but some required regular trips to Chicago and a few to California.

I also made two trips to Germany while with Siemens. After one of them I vacationed with my wife in England where, among other things, we toured Wembley Stadium, the iconic London venue which has hosted many historic soccer matches. The best meal my wife and I had on that vacation was at a Greek café near the bed and breakfast we stayed in while visiting Eastwood. But 1985 was years before London became the international culinary center it is today.

My Siemens boss taught me the importance of wearing good suits and eating at fine restaurants. The executive also challenged me to bring the department into the computer age. I responded by commissioning a network of Apple Macintosh computers and peripherals, which was rare in the corporate world during the late 1980s. Many of the best people I've ever worked with during my career were colleagues at Siemens. I organized a reunion for our department members in 2005 and remain in touch with some of them.

Nobody I met at Siemens were nicer gentlemen than two Cuban refugees who I would occasionally travel to Chicago and Cherry Hill, New Jersey, to meet. One was a pipe-smoking soft-spoken business manager whose family left Cuba for California when he was a boy. With almost no trace of an accent, he told me about the best Cuban restaurant in Chicago, which I ate at more than once. The other was an older business manager who left Cuba after attending college there. His memory of pre-Castro Cuba was "everyone just wanted to have fun." He left Cuba and married a Puerto Rican woman with whom he had two daughters. His accent remained strong enough after living in the U.S. for almost twenty-five years that I once asked him to repeat himself a few times over lunch after I heard him keep saying "bif" rather than "beef." These were the first two Cuban senior businessmen I met, and they set the bar high for other businessmen, including me.

After the in-house agency was disbanded and I assumed a less interesting role, I left Siemens to join Engelhard, a specialty minerals and precious metals company just down the street at the Metro Park commercial complex in Iselin, New Jersey. Engelhard recruited me aggressively, offering me a significant pay raise to handle advertising and other business communication responsibilities for its paper pigments division. That lasted less than a year and a half before, with my wife pregnant with our second child in 1990, my position was eliminated as part of what companies typically refer to as a "reorganization."

Next, I worked as the general manager for the Eagles Soccerplex and Meadowlands Tennis Club in Carlstadt, New Jersey. It was an interesting but ultimately unsuccessful venture in which four business partners who owned the New Jersey Eagles of the American Professional Soccer League (which I was the part-time public relations director of one season) replaced half of the tennis courts in the Meadowlands Tennis Club with an artificial turf soccer pitch. The club succeeded in attracting soccer teams—many of them with Hispanic players—to compete in its leagues for a fee in the winter, but not during other times of the year. Meanwhile, tennis players at the club became increasingly unhappy with sharing a locker room and other parts of the facility with the very different patrons there to play soccer.

I was in charge of the staff and the club's operations, including paying the bills, during my year as its general manager. I had never run a business before—the owners offered me the job because of my corporate experience and the good public relations work I did for their soccer team—but I caught on quickly. A valuable lesson I learned while there was that almost everything is negotiable. The local utility once threatened to turn off our power for falling behind on payments, but I was able to convince them not to by speaking with their service technician and handing him a small check. There were plenty of other service providers and potential customers I needed to negotiate with during my year there to keep the club operating.

Among the interesting people I met while at the soccer and tennis club was a new Cuban immigrant who worked as a handyman for a short while. He was quite resourceful and able to fix broken doors with a butter knife and do other repairs without the proper tools, just as he had probably been forced to do while in Cuba only few months earlier.

I soon realized I needed to find a better position to utilize my strongest professional skills and support my family. For the second time in two years, my career was in transition. During that time, a human resources manager for a pharmaceutical company whose daughter was friends with my wife suggested I think about changing my name back to Lopez. With more major companies paying attention to their EEO (equal employment opportunity) practices and statistics, he thought a Hispanic surname would make me more appealing to prospective employers. I did not for a moment consider his suggestion because I had been using the Bruns name for over twenty years at that point. Besides, I wanted to get a new job on merit and not just because a company was trying to improve its EEO numbers.

In the summer of 1991, I landed a marketing communication position at Rhone-Poulenc, a France-based specialty chemicals company. After I had been there for a few years, a human resources executive was quite happy to hear I was a Cuban American. When I responded affirmatively to his question about whether I had indicated this on the EEO paperwork all employees were asked to complete, he fist-pumped and exclaimed, "Yes!"

During the fifteen years between 1991-2006 I worked at the specialty chemicals company, my role changed every two or three years. For a period in the mid-1990s, I was the manager of a division's communications department. We functioned as an in-house crisis communication, public affairs, internal communication, media relations, marketing communication and graphics services agency. When Rhone-Poulenc was spun off into different companies and the part I was in became known as Rhodia, I eventually became the global communication director for its pharmaceutical ingredients and services division and director of communication for all North American operations.

I made dozens of trips to France while at Rhone-Poulenc and Rhodia. A majority of the trips were to Paris, but I also went to Lyon and other parts of the country. I remember on more than one occasion that my departure gate at Paris Charles de Gaulle Airport was not far from the gate for flights to Havana. I sometimes strolled over to see who was flying off to Cuba and imagined myself waiting to board a flight to Havana one day. I am still waiting for the right time to do that.

At one point, when I was one of only two Americans in the pharmaceutical ingredients enterprise's worldwide management team, it was strongly suggested I learn French. I tried. Despite taking weekly lessons and doing my homework, the beautiful language did not come easily to me. My French teacher once observed that I spoke French with a Spanish accent, which was amusing since I did not even speak English with a Spanish accent.

At one point, I thought my French language skills were halfway decent. When I landed in Paris on one of my trips, I told the taxicab driver which hotel to take me to in French. When it was obvious he—a northern African immigrant like many Parisian cab drivers at the time—didn't understand what I was saying, I took out my itinerary and showed him where I wanted to go. I slumped in my seat, frustrated at my failure to communicate such basic information in French. A few hours later, I explained what happened to a French colleague. He tried to make me feel better by saying, "Don't worry, Charley, they don't understand us either."

I felt like a citizen of the world who just happened to have a U.S. passport during the years I frequently traveled to France. I didn't think I fit the stereotype many Europeans have of Americans, which I heard was that we are loud and overweight (although most of the American colleagues I travelled on business with were neither). When I was in Lyon one day, though, I couldn't help but notice the stares I was getting while walking around the streets for some post-travel exercise. I asked a French colleague that evening why people might have been staring at me. He said it was probably because I looked American, and he went on to describe at length how every stitch of clothing I wore and even my hair style was unlike anything a Frenchman would wear. So much for being a citizen of the world who just happened to have a U.S. passport!

There was one block of hours I spent in Lyon, though, where I looked like I fit right in. On June 21, 1998, I was among 39,100 soccer fans packed in the Stade de Gerland to see the U.S. men's national soccer team play Iran in the World Cup. Held nearly twenty years after the Iranian Revolution overthrew the pro-Western Shah of Iran and the subsequent U.S. support of Iraq in its war with Iran, this match had huge political undertones. Almost everyone in the stadium was either American or pro-American. Many of the Iranians in the stands were political exiles and very friendly to the U.S. fans sitting around them. The only hostilities I noticed were between the anti-Islamic regime exiles and the few Iranian citizens in attendance. To my huge disappointment, the U.S. lost the match, 2-1. But what I will remember most about that day was how well everyone got along inside and outside of the stadium in Lyon. Many years later, I read a quote from a U.S. player stating, "We did more in 90 minutes than the politicians did in 20 years."

One of the people who impressed me the most during my fifteen years at the company was an Argentina-born executive who could speak Portuguese, French, Italian and German fluently along with Spanish and English. He had lots of energy and panache and little patience for those who lacked his level of motivation. I felt honored to be in the circle of co-workers he trusted and was comfortable to be with. He shared an outlook on work and life that I appreciated. And he sometimes drove a Mazda Miata, one of my favorite cars over the years.

There was a Cuban American accountant that worked on my floor for a couple of years who I got to know. A shy, unassuming heavyset man and heavy smoker, he had young cousins who had left Cuba as part of Operation *Pedro Pan*, the covert operation run by Father Bryan O. Walsh of the Catholic Welfare Bureau that brought 14,048 unaccompanied Cuban children to the U.S. during the early 1960s. He did not grow up in New Jersey and was not familiar with the large Cuban American neighborhood in Hudson County. I therefore suggested we take a long lunch at one of my favorite cafés on Bergenline Avenue in Union City. He was ecstatic to join me and ordered his lunch and *cortadito* coffee in perfect Spanish. A few weeks later, his boss thanked me for taking him out to lunch.

I also met a woman while at Rhone-Poulenc who in some ways seemed less Cuban than me but in other ways was much more so. She was Jewish with a Polish surname and said her family fled Europe during the Nazi occupation and the Holocaust. In heavily accented English, she told me she grew up in Cuba speaking Spanish, liking Cuban food, and enjoying the dances that were popular on the island during the 1950s. Like nearly all Jewish people in Cuba, she and her family left after Fidel Castro seized power and imposed an oppressive Communist government.

In the 1990s, when cigar smoking experienced a resurgence in popularity, I took advantage of my trips to France to smuggle home some Havana cigars. The United States had forbidden these pleasures to be imported for over thirty years by this point. I never felt more Cuban than when I smoked a Romeo y Julieta, Cohiba or Montecristo on the porch of my Robbinsville, New Jersey, home. During a business function where a bunch of guys sat around smoking, one of my colleagues commented how "natural" I looked with a cigar in my hand. "Of course he does," someone chimed in. "He's Cuban!"

In 2007 I joined the Novartis generic pharmaceuticals division, Sandoz, in Princeton as director of U.S. communication. Within two years I moved on to work in Novartis' New York City U.S. corporate headquarters as director of corporate reputation. While there, I initiated the development of the company's first *YouTube* channel, among other accomplishments. I also rediscovered my love for the city of my birth and childhood. From 2008 to 2012, I commuted from my Robbinsville home to my New York City office three or four days a week. During most of that time, my office was located on Fifth Avenue next to Rockefeller Center. I was excited to be able to see part of the big Rockefeller Center Christmas tree every December from my window. For my final months of employment, my office was a few blocks east on Park Avenue, inside the New York Central Railroad building also known as the Helmsley building.

I made it a point to get outside almost every lunch hour I worked in New York. As much as I liked my job, being out for lunch was typically the highlight of my day. I frequented all the Cuban cafés within a short walking distance. The couple of Sophie's Cuban Cuisine spots nearby and the Margon Restaurant on West 46 Street were my favorites. I also discovered dozens of other cafés and delis where I could enjoy a tasty and reasonable meal—often a salad so that I could also maintain my weight—while people watching.

While working in New York City, I often stepped inside Saint Patrick's Cathedral to pray for my good fortune in life, usually on the mornings my commuter bus dropped me off earlier than usual. A couple of times a year I would extend my lunch hour with a walk to my old Amsterdam Houses neighborhood. Sometimes I would walk to the Church of Saint Paul the Apostle, sit in a pew, and look around the inside of the church while memories of childhood Sunday mornings raced around my mind. I thought of how I used to sit with my classmates and when I received my First Holy Communion. I remembered how nicely everyone dressed on Easter Sunday.

The tourists and crowds around midtown Manhattan rarely bothered me. I soaked up the sights and began sharing my observations every day I was in the city on *Twitter*. Only rainy days and the ensuing "umbrella wars" prevented me from enjoying the streets of the city the years I worked there. On those days, I typically retreated to the subway in order to get back to the Port Authority Bus Terminal or Penn Station for my ride back home. The commute didn't bother me. I told those who asked I looked forward to being in two places I liked: the city during the day, and at home in the evening. Perhaps I might have felt differently if I did not have the flexibility to work from home one or two days a week.

My New York City work situation did not last as long as I would have liked. Organizational changes in 2012 led to the elimination of my position as director of executive and internal communication, in which I oversaw the major update of the company's intranet portal and initiated development of a mobile app for employees. By the end of the same year, the department I had belonged to and other positions within the corporate organization were eliminated. By that time in my career, I was part of two minority groups: Latin Americans working in corporate communication, and males fifty and over working in the field. Corporate communication professionals by then were mostly young and female.

The "Young Star" had turned into the "Old Guy."

I succeeded in landing interviews with many major companies in the New Jersey/New York City area when I attempted to get my corporate communication career back on track during 2012-13. But for the first time, I received no offers for permanent full-time work. A recruiter whose opinion I respected told me, "Charley, nobody out there is looking to bring men in their mid-fifties into their company. You've done some consulting assignments. You should learn to love consulting."

I have learned to like consulting. When clients keep me busy, I love it. I've landed many interesting assignments, mostly with pharmaceutical companies, and worked with many wonderful people who appreciate the value of my skills and experience, particularly when their organization is in transition or has a special need. I've succeeded in providing ideas, words, and solutions to help organizations meet challenges. Among other things, I've helped company leaders effectively articulate talking points to associates and external audiences, and crafted communication plans and other strategic documents that have ensured communication efforts align with key organizational messages. My client assignments have also enabled me to utilize and expand my knowledge of new and emerging communication technologies.

I also took advantage of the opportunity to share my professional knowledge and experiences with undergraduate students as an adjunct professor at Monmouth University in West Long Branch and a couple of other New Jersey colleges. It was a little strange, although not too uncomfortable, to be called "Professor" by students younger than my own children.

It took a few years after my last permanent full-time job, but I realize I am doing what I want and need to do at this point of my career and this station in my life. After nearly thirty-five years of getting steady paychecks, benefits, and paid time off, it was an adjustment to be self-employed. But I enjoy the greater freedom I have now to make my own hours and handle a wider variety of work and challenges while working from home. I look forward to visiting my clients periodically, but I don't miss the daily commute to an office.

The name of the limited liability company I established for my consultancy is Charles Anthony Communication. I chose to use the first and middle names I was born with and never changed. Including my legal surname, even though it's the one I've used throughout my career, just did not feel right to me. And including the last name on my original birth certificate did not seem appropriate.

The Young Star in Europe, 1986

Chapter 15. The Husband: Love and Marriage

I met my future wife, Noreen, in 1976, through a mutual friend while I was a sophomore in college. A good friend of mine and two high school girls picked me up from home after work one evening in his Ford Mustang and we drove to the Star Tavern in Orange, New Jersey. We drank beer—the legal drinking age was only 18 at the time—and ate pizza, but I could not take my eyes off his blonde-haired blue-eyed date. I admit to also flirting with the red-haired girl my friend meant to be my date that night.

I dated the tall, red-haired girl for a few months. When my friend stopped dating the blonde I could not stop thinking about that summer, I called to invite her to an Elton John concert at Madison Square Garden. Her mother answered the phone and gladly accepted the invitation on behalf of her daughter. The mom knew me from being around their house with my previous girlfriend and, according to Noreen, thought I was a nice guy. She also figured that, since I was a student at a private college who owned two Ford Thunderbirds and lived in one of the newest houses in Bloomfield, I had some money. I hope I didn't prove she was wrong about being a nice guy, although she soon realized I wasn't exactly wealthy.

Noreen and I dated during my last two years in college. During that time, I accompanied her to her high school prom. Within a year of falling in love, I started a photo album with favorite pictures I had taken of her. Decades later I was reminded of just how smitten I was by my teenage girlfriend when I came across the following typewritten words on a yellowed sheet of paper:

"If the warmth inside a woman's soul could ever be reflected accurately by her physical beauty, then the softness of her peaceful blue eyes and the tenderness of her innocent smile instantly announce the tranquility and contentment which lies inside her heart. Looking at her, I see everything in life which is positive; knowing her I feel everything about life which is inspiring.

"Her blonde hair suggests elegance and finesse when it is curled or combed in a professional manner. When it flows down the side of her soft face, it suggests honesty and sincerity. The roundish shape of her face implies wholeness; with makeup it insinuates an impressive air of sophistication, without it it recommends a refreshing simplicity. Her well-proportioned figure suggests a happiness that is real and lived. Indeed, to actually see her beauty is to experience her happiness. To know her beauty is to feel a soul which bubbles joyfully."

In December of 1979, after she had been working full-time for two years and I for over a year, I asked Noreen to marry me. I was smitten not only by her outward beauty but also by her kindness and our compatibility, even though our family backgrounds and professional interests were quite different. She shared my interest in sports and the variety of music I enjoyed. We both enjoyed visiting New York City and drinking good coffee or, sometimes, imbibing in something stronger.

I was happy to discover her family's culinary tastes and have fun with them. That included dining in restaurants, taking long rides, going to Atlantic City and other places I was unfamiliar with and regularly whooping it up at parties with their extended family and friends. Her family's idea of fun was more festive than my mother and stepfather's idea of a good time.

One winter evening, after a cup of strong coffee from a favorite café near her home, Noreen and I went for a ride to Brookdale Park on the border of Montclair and Bloomfield. A light snow had just fallen, which made the park prettier than usual. When I parked the car in the lot by the running track, she got out and proceeded to carve a big heart with our initials inside the freshly fallen snow on the grass field with her feet. Her spontaneity touched me. On my way to work the following morning, I stopped by the stands overlooking the running track to search for her artwork, which was still visible. It was just one of many days she brought a big smile to my face and much joy to my heart.

With my career and our relationship continuing to blossom, Noreen and I married in June of 1981. Her parents were Roman Catholic and wanted us to marry in the local Catholic church, Saint Thomas the Apostle. I had no problem with that, but my stepfather asked that a Lutheran minister also be present for the wedding ceremony. To appease him, my fiancée and I agreed. More importantly, my future in-laws and Saint Thomas the Apostle Church went along with the request.

My wife is half Italian, a quarter Irish, and a quarter mix of Eastern European, including Slovak. Her parents are arguably the oddest couple I know. My mother-in-law, a first generation American whose parents came to New Jersey from southern Italy, loved to cook and eat all kinds of food for many years but never drank too much alcohol. Like many women of her generation, sports did not interest her. My father-in-law, on the other hand, is the fussiest eater I know. There seems little logic to what he likes and dislikes on his plate, which must have taken his wife some time to figure out. I'm sure she realized pretty quickly, though, that he enjoyed drinking and gambling, interests he told me years later ran in his family. He was also a sports fanatic in his younger days. Love makes strange bedfellows, I've heard it said, and that is certainly true of my in-laws. From what I have seen, they've remained blissfully in love for over sixty years and have shared that love with their three children and eight grandchildren.

Like most people I knew in Bloomfield, my future in-laws only knew of two Cubans: Ricky Ricardo and Fidel Castro. Although I had long tired of the Ricky Ricardo imitations and references, I was glad they didn't harp on Fidel Castro like some others often did. I hope I've made a good impression on them about Cuban Americans over the years. For sure, my mother-in-law has enjoyed the Cuban food her daughter has learned to prepare.

And my father-in-law? He won't even try Cuban food, except for the one time he reluctantly ate a single black bean with a disparaging look on his face.

Noreen said my passion for sports was one of the reasons she was attracted to me. As the first child of a man who thoroughly enjoyed sports, she grew up going to sporting events with her father. They attended New York Mets baseball games, New York Giants football games and New York Rangers hockey and New York Knicks basketball games together when she was a young girl. She told me that she wasn't interested in boys who didn't like sports, so my being a sports fan and sportswriter for a daily newspaper appealed to her.

The feeling was mutual. A few months after we began dating, her father gave us tickets to see a Giants football game at their new stadium in the Meadowlands. It was the first time I attended a National Football League game. The following year we returned to Giants Stadium to see our first New York Cosmos soccer game, which featured the great Pele. We got hooked on the sport and team and after attending more games that season and the following year, we bought a pair of Cosmos season tickets. From 1979 to 1985, when the team ceased operations after the North American Soccer League folded, we rarely missed a Cosmos game. To this day, we have wonderful memories of those soccer games and players we saw at the Meadowlands.

I observed a lot about Latin American culture and people at the Sunday afternoon and occasional weeknight evening soccer games we attended during those years. Soccer had never been very popular in Cuba or among Cuban Americans. In the lead-up to the 1962 Cuban Missile Crisis, that indifference tipped off U.S. intelligence officials to the growing Soviet Union presence on the island. They noted the dramatic increase in the number of soccer fields around the island, especially by military sites. These soccer fields were being used by Soviet Union military personnel, not Cubans, it was accurately determined.

Many South American and Central American immigrants attended those Meadowlands Cosmos soccer games. When the Cosmos hosted reigning World Cup champions Argentina on a summer night in 1979, the stadium was packed with over 60,000 Argentina fans. Three years later, when the Peru national team played the Cosmos as part of a pre-World Cup tour, the stadium held over 40,000 Peru fans on a cold and windy Sunday afternoon. Brazilian, Chilean, and Columbian fans also regularly came to the stadium for soccer matches, as did many Mexican fans. I'm sure, though, there were very few Cuban Americans in attendance. Even many years later, when the Cuban national team played in the Meadowlands stadium as part of an international doubleheader, Noreen and I noticed that Cuban fans—some encouraging Cuba's players to defect while they were in the U.S.—were few compared with other Caribbean and Central American national team fans in attendance.

While I started working full-time and becoming acquainted with Noreen's family, I lived in Bloomfield with my mother, stepfather, younger brother, and sister. I paid room and board and followed my stepfather's rules for three years before getting married and moving into a two-family house in neighboring Clifton, New Jersey with my bride. I looked into moving to an apartment with a friend a few months after graduating college, but decided I preferred to stay with my two young siblings and save some money before getting married.

Although I didn't ask her to, Noreen took on the Bruns surname after we married. It was traditional then—and still is—for a wife to take on her husband's name in the U.S. But she did tell me a few years later that she would have been hesitant to use the Lopez name if I hadn't changed it. Hispanics were still few and far between within her family's Bloomfield and Clifton circles and she only knew of one Cuban American in her high school. She would not have been comfortable as "a Lopez" at the time. In hindsight, I don't think it would have mattered to me if my surname was Lopez and she didn't want to take on the name. It was never a custom I felt strongly about.

Getting married and starting our life together in Clifton in 1981 was among the many good decisions my wife and I have made over the years. We rented an apartment in a Wellington Street, Clifton two-family house for four years. Another newlywed couple lived in the apartment upstairs and quickly became among our best friends. By 1985, Noreen and I were in a financial position to buy our first house.

With the help of my stepfather—he had become a part-time realtor to supplement his teaching income by that time—we found a fifty-year-old three-bedroom house that was right for us on a 33'x100' plot of land on Elston Street in Bloomfield. We would live just a few blocks from the Birch Street home my stepfather and mother purchased in 1969 and our family lived in for six years. It was a bit of déjà vu for me to walk some of the same streets and frequent the stores and neighborhood park that were part of my adolescence.

Noreen and I started our family and enjoyed living in our Bloomfield house for almost nine years. During this time, she completed her college studies while continuing to work part-time. I attempted to write my first book while living in that house. A few days a week for a couple of months, I would wake up early in the morning, make a strong cup of *café con leche* and for about an hour bang out words about the life of a fictional Hispanic person from New York City on my Apple 2c computer. Then I would commute to my office job. After outlining the story and writing over a hundred pages, I abandoned the book project. I just wasn't happy with it. When I retrieved the manuscript nearly thirty years later to see if parts of it could be salvaged for a short story, I was reminded why I had abandoned it in the first place. I put it away again.

There was another "Hispanic" family just a couple of doors away from our Elston Street house: an Argentine family who seemed to have more in common with the Italian immigrants across the street. That should have been no surprise to me since I've read the number of Italians who have immigrated to Argentina since the middle of the 19th century is much greater than the number from Spain. Even though Argentina is a former colony of Spain that retains Spanish as its official language, it is the country with the highest number of Italian immigrants in the world. Perhaps that explains why I can never quite understand the Spanish language spoken by Argentines!

A year after I began working in Cranbury, New Jersey in 1991, Noreen and I agreed it made good sense for us to move closer to my job, a decision which understandably disappointed my stepfather and mother. To appease him, I asked my stepfather to help sell our Bloomfield home. It was a decision I came to regret because he did not seem motivated to help facilitate my family's departure from his hometown. It took over a year to land a buyer, and that deal fell through. Finally, in the summer of 1994, we moved over an hour and a half south to Robbinsville, New Jersey, which was just twenty minutes from my office.

Moving to a newly constructed four-bedroom house on half an acre in the Windsor Meadows neighborhood of Robbinsville turned out to be a great decision for our family. We made many new friends and, most importantly, it enabled me to spend a few more hours each weekday with my family rather than on the New Jersey Turnpike and Garden

State Parkway fighting traffic. I was able to be part of the soccer, baseball and other sports activities of our sons Steven and Kevin, who were born in 1986 and 1990, respectively, often as a coach. I was also able to participate in their Cub Scouts and Boy Scouts activities and be present for nearly all their school events. I also spent a lot of time with them in our back yard and inside our big home during the eighteen years we lived in Robbinsville.

There was only one other Hispanic family in our new Robbinsville neighborhood and, for a short period of time, a Hispanic man of mixed Black and white ancestry (often referred to as "*mulato*") who was married to a white woman. There were also a few Asian Indian families, including a couple who moved next door with her parents and became friends with us as they raised a family. Otherwise, the neighborhood—indeed, the whole town—was the least diverse place I have ever lived. Still, I've often said it was a great place for my wife and I to raise our children.

Four years after our eldest son graduated college, just as our youngest son was preparing to start his senior year, I lost my full-time job with Novartis in New York City. Noreen and I made the quick decision to sell our Robbinsville house and live year-round in the beachfront condo we had purchased as a second home a few years earlier in Long Branch, a city on the Jersey Shore. We're quite comfortable in our two-bedroom Long Branch unit, which we hope to call home for the rest of our lives.

Long Branch is certainly the most diverse place I've resided since living in New York City. The population of Long Branch is 51 percent white, 30 percent Hispanic and 13 percent Black, according to U.S. Census Bureau estimates published by *Census Reporter* in 2018. My sense is that most of the city's Hispanic population is Mexican, Central American and Puerto Rican. There are also many Brazilians in Long Branch.

Although they are often considered Latinos, Brazilians are technically not Hispanic since they speak Portuguese rather than Spanish. But my Brazilian barber in the West End neighborhood of Long Branch and many of his shop's patrons do remind me of many Hispanics I've met.

In any case, I don't believe many of the city's approximately 30,000 population are of Cuban heritage, but I do feel as if I've come full circle in Long Branch. Today, my home is just a few steps from a beach, as it was in Cuba for a few years, in a town where Spanish—and other non-English languages—are often heard and diversity is plentiful, like in my former New York City neighborhood. I have also returned to the Roman Catholic church after being Lutheran for nearly forty-five years since my stepfather and mother were married. Noreen and I are very comfortable walking to Saint Michael's Church on Ocean Avenue by Takanassee Lake in Long Branch on Sundays, just as I felt when I lived in New York and walked to Church of Saint Paul the Apostle on Columbus Avenue to worship with my neighbors and classmates.

The city of Long Branch has a fascinating history. For this reason, I was motivated to write a poem, "The Friendly City: No Vacancy," about its past and present. I posted my 118-line history about the city on my blog, *1400 Characters*, in 2019 and read it at the Brighton Bar just a few blocks from my home that September.

The nine story, 115-unit building on Ocean Avenue in the West End neighborhood of Long Branch called Harbour Mansion where my wife and I live also has a fascinating history. When neighbors started telling me stories about our building's past, I didn't know what to believe. During 2016-17, for the fun of it, I researched, wrote, and published an eleven-part blog series about the history of the building. It turns out some of what I heard is true, and some is not. I also discovered information about our building nearly all my neighbors had forgotten or never knew. At the invitation of the Long Branch Historical Association, I delivered a presentation about the history of Harbour Mansion in front of a receptive audience at the Long Branch Free Public Library in March of 2017.

Long Branch also holds a fleeting place in Cuban baseball history. In 1913, the Long Branch Cubans became the first U.S. minor league baseball team composed almost entirely of Cubans, according to the Jorge S. Figueredo book, *Cuban Baseball: A Statistical History, 1878-1961*. Because of low attendances at their games, the team moved out of Long Branch after the 1915 season.

Through the years, as we've moved to new homes and raised a family, I've been fortunate to have Noreen as my partner. Like many married couples, of course, our relationship has had some ups and downs. My family's history is littered with failed and bad marriages. Unlike my parents, though, we always managed to work things out. And, unlike my mother and stepfather, our relationship has grown stronger over the years. Perhaps my in-laws provided their children a good example of how love can persevere and blossom in a marriage. My wife has stood by me during the past forty years, tolerating my imperfections and giving me enough space to continue growing personally and professionally during my sometimes less-than-smooth journey through life.

Noreen and I are happier than ever to be together. She's always been sweet, industrious, and courageous, traits I associated with Abuela Belen. I believe my wife feels we're an ideal partnership for the golden years that, God willing, await us. And, after experiencing some Hispanic culture with me and observing the growing presence of Latinos in New Jersey and other parts of the U.S., she says she likely would have taken on the Lopez name by now if it had still been my surname.

The Husband with Noreen, 1981

Chapter 16. The Father: Blessed by God

By the time I was thirty years old, I knew that what I wanted to do more than anything else in life was to be a good father. In the autumn of 1986, after a difficult pregnancy, Noreen blessed us by delivering a healthy son, Steven. I was there when he was born and believe I've remained there for him all his life. Because I was very grateful for Steven's birth after almost losing him early in my wife's pregnancy, I sometimes felt I couldn't do enough for him. I changed his diapers, fed him, and laid him down to sleep when I was home from work. I held Steven in my arms on the couch of our living room during much of the New York Mets' 1986 World Series triumph over the Boston Red Sox. I held Steven so much, Noreen's grandmother thought I was spoiling him. Noreen and I didn't think that was possible, but we did notice Steven rarely crawled. When he was nearly a year old, Steven went from mostly being in our arms to standing up on the floor and taking his first steps!

During Steven's pre-school years, I often ran errands with him on Saturday mornings in the two-seater 1985 Pontiac Fiero my wife and I bought a few months after moving into our Bloomfield house. We still have it to this day. I would strap Steven in his baby car seat in the front with me and shift the manual transmission Fiero around Bloomfield and Clifton streets for an hour or two, stopping at a favorite delicatessen, dairy store, film and photo processing shop and wherever else we needed to go while Noreen attended college classes or worked. I have fond memories of listening to Felix Hernandez on WBGO-FM radio while on those Saturday morning errands. But—even though it was legal then and is legal now—can you imagine the outcry these days over a father driving a sporty plastic-body two-seater car around town with a child in the front next to him?!?

For a few years in the late 1980s, Noreen and I were convinced Steven would be an only child. But thanks to advances in medication to treat Noreen's ulcerative colitis, we were blessed with a second healthy son, Kevin, in the autumn of 1990. Grateful for our good fortune, we decided not to press our luck expanding our family further. Kevin was a perfect baby who enabled us to meet the challenge of equally caring for and loving two young children. I spent as much time changing Kevin's diapers, feeding him and laying him down to sleep as I had with his brother. Steven was excited to have a sibling and didn't seem to mind sharing his parents' attention.

Kevin also liked riding in the '85 Pontiac Fiero with me occasionally, although we could never have his brother with us since the car only had two seats. As Kevin grew up, he was more anxious to drive that little car than Steven seemed to be. When Kevin was about twenty years old, he sent me a photograph of him driving the same Fiero for the very first time. I was riding a bus home from my New York City office when the photo arrived on my phone, and I grinned from ear to ear.

I have countless wonderful memories of my two sons over the years. Among them are the many New York Jets football games I attended with one or the other for fifteen years. We were thrilled to obtain a pair of season tickets in time for the 1996 season, during which Steven turned ten years old and Kevin six. I tailgated in the Meadowlands parking lot with one of my sons before almost every Jets home game and we were always in our seats for the opening kick-off and through the final whistle. I was very grateful that each of my sons enjoyed the football games with me. They acted excited to be there with their father and never nagged me.

There was one Jets game Steven and I almost left early. Almost. It was a Monday night—October 23, 2000, to be exact. He needed to be in school the next morning and I had to be at work. The thought therefore crossed my mind that we might want to get home by midnight. The Jets were losing, 30-7, at the end of the third quarter. I suggested to Steven we wait to see what the Jets did with their first possession in the last quarter before deciding whether to go home or stay. In a little over a minute of play, the Jets scored a touchdown. Four minutes later, they scored another. We stayed in our seats to watch them win a thriller in overtime, 40-37. We didn't get home until the wee hours of the morning, but we were glad to witness the "Monday Night Miracle" in person.

Kevin was also a bit of a good luck charm at sporting events. In one instance, he brought us good luck before we even took our seats. After being away most of the week on a business trip to France, I promised Kevin we would go to a rare Seton Hall basketball game at Walsh Auditorium when I got back. The Pirates would play only a game or two on the South Orange campus before hosting opponents at the Meadowlands Arena. As we pulled into the school parking lot listening to the pre-game broadcast, we heard the announcer say the game was sold out. That was a big surprise to me, and a big problem for the two of us since I had not purchased tickets in advance. I suggested we go to the box office anyway just in case a pair of unclaimed tickets somehow became available. A man behind us in line overheard me talking about the situation to Kevin, who was not more than ten years old. He offered us two of his four tickets, explaining they had been given to him by the monsignor who was president of the university, and refused to accept money. Kevin and I could not believe our good luck and we thoroughly enjoyed the game from our complimentary seats.

My experiences at Jets football games, Seton Hall basketball games, New York Mets baseball games and New York/New Jersey MetroStars soccer games with my sons were very different than the occasional baseball game I would attend with my stepfather while I was growing up. My stepfather acted bored at those games, as though he had done me a favor by bringing me. And of course, I had to express my gratitude to him. He sometimes brought a newspaper with him to the stadium and, to my annoyance when he finished reading it, would do something immature like tossing peanut shells at fans seated rows in front of us to see how they would react. This elementary schoolteacher was particularly amused when an annoyed fan would turn around to see who might have tossed the shell. In hindsight, knowing what I understand now about him, he was likely annoyed that I seemed more interested in the game than him. Not surprisingly, by the time I started high school I had no desire to continue attending baseball games with my stepfather. I took a bus and subway by myself to see a midweek game at Yankee Stadium with about 5,000 other diehard baseball fans in April of 1972, just after a strike delayed the start of the season.

My two sons carry the Bruns name, of course, but don't have an ounce of German or Bruns blood in them. They are each half Cuban, one quarter Italian, one eighth Irish and one eighth Eastern European. Up until their high school years they were blond-haired and didn't look one bit like stereotypical Cubans. They still don't, even as their hair has darkened as adults. Then again, their paternal great grandmother—Abuela Belen—was blonde. It is another example of how stereotypes are often inaccurate. It's not unusual for Spaniards, especially those from the northern part of the country, to be blond. Since interracial marriages in Cuba before the 1959 Revolution were not as common as in Puerto Rico, it is not rare for Cuban Americans to have fair hair as well as fair skin. And, as Noreen reminds me, her mother—our sons' maternal grandmother—and her grandfather had also been blond when they were younger.

I always wanted my two sons to know about my Cuban roots and, despite our Bruns surname, the Lopez side of our family. On a hot summer day when they were about thirteen and nine years old, Steven and Kevin accompanied me and Noreen for the first time to the Amsterdam Houses neighborhood in New York City where I had spent much of my childhood. I pointed out the apartment I lived in as a child with my mother and Lou, their grandmother and uncle. I showed them the playgrounds I frequented. They may not have appreciated until that day just how different my upbringing was from theirs. A few hours later, we went to the New York Transit Museum in Brooklyn (by subway, of course) and they saw how excited their father was to see the old trains and related exhibits, many which brought back wonderful memories to me.

My mother was undoubtedly the clearest reminder my sons had of their Cuban ancestry. She loved all her grandchildren but got to spend the most time with Steven and Kevin. Her strong Spanish accent was probably the only one they heard for many years, and no doubt my sons overheard their grandmother and father talk about Cuba and the possibility of returning there together for vacation one year, which sadly never happened. She smiled and laughed a lot with her grandchildren around, and also gave Steven and Kevin reasons to smile and laugh a lot when they were together. My mother and stepfather hosted my children in their North Wildwood vacation unit once or twice annually for over ten years, usually although not always with Noreen and me. I think Steven and Kevin will always fondly remember how much their grandmother enjoyed riding bicycles on the Wildwood boardwalk with them in the morning.

I raised my two sons to regard my stepfather as their grandfather. Their biological paternal grandfather, Humberto, was never part of their lives. My father passed away in Florida when my first son was only six months old. His sister, Tía Gloria, gave him a photo of me holding Steven before he died, so he left the world knowing he had a grandson from both of his children. But he was a biological grandfather who Steven and Kevin only saw a handful of photos of and heard a few stories about years later. My stepfather was the paternal grandfather who, along with my mother and Noreen's parents, helped celebrate birthdays, Christmases, and other special family events with them. He was the grandfather who sometimes watched or did fun things with them when Noreen and I needed a babysitter so she could attend her college classes, or we could occasionally go out or take on a house project alone. My stepfather always seemed willing to "help out" Noreen and me if it involved being with our sons. He clearly liked the company of children. It was several years into their childhood before Steven and Kevin realized "Grandpa Bruns" was not actually their biological grandfather.

The relationship my children had with my stepfather while growing up was healthy for them. It was equally good for my stepfather, especially after my kids didn't need to have their diapers changed. He enjoyed talking to Steven and Kevin about their schooling and watching them play organized sports or participate in school or other activities, like many grandparents do.

But my stepfather was never content to just be a proud observer at my children's activities. He always needed to let Steven and Kevin know he was there and what he thought of their game, event, or other activity. I don't recall him ever taking a picture of my children—my mother and I took plenty of them, he probably reasoned—but I do remember he wanted to be in many of them, as my photo albums and home video collection prove. I also remember how much he enjoyed telling me about the candy and junk food he typically gave Steven and Kevin, even though he knew very well Noreen and I were trying our best to provide them a healthy diet. My sister pointed out to me the same enjoyment he used to get reporting to her how he broke "rules" like this with her daughter.

As Noreen and I were raising Steven and Kevin, I began to realize more and more often that I was referencing experiences with my biological father and stepfather for guidance on what NOT to do with my own children. It's ironic but true. When I came across a situation with my children for the first time and needed to figure out the right thing to do or say, I thought back to what my biological father didn't do, or my stepfather did, and typically proceeded to do the OPPOSITE.

Take Christmastime, for example. I don't remember my biological father ever giving me a gift. Also, it was unusual for me to receive exactly what I asked for, no matter how modest it was, once my stepfather and mother married. Unsurprisingly, Noreen and I tried our best to give Steven and Kevin exactly what they wanted every Christmas while they were growing up while also helping them understand the true meaning of Christmas. We did this by making sure we continued attending church through the Advent season, including on Christmas Eve or Christmas morning.

When Lou and I were living with our divorced mother in New York City, we enjoyed decorating our silver artificial tree every Christmas. Looking at pictures of it now, I realize it was not exactly the fullest, most attractive of Christmas trees, but it was relatively stylish at the time in our neighborhood. More importantly, it was our family's tree and very special to the three of us. Imagine our hurt, therefore, when our future stepfather first saw the tree and mocked it. He declared it would not be part of our Christmas in the future. Sure enough, we had real Christmas trees that he picked out from that point on. It also hurt Lou and me to hear the criticism we received every Christmas over how we decorated the tree with tinsel and ornaments. Our stepfather would berate us if we didn't place ornaments or strands of tinsel exactly where he thought they should be. Predictably, after a few years we didn't want anything to do with the family Christmas tree.

Remembering this experience with my stepfather, Noreen and I allowed our children to place ornaments wherever they wanted as soon as they became interested in helping decorate our Christmas tree. We encouraged Steven and Kevin to put up the decorations they made at their elementary school or Sunday School class and wanted them to feel the family tree was as much theirs as it was ours to enjoy.

Christmas Eve was typically an exhausting holiday for Noreen and me, especially once we started hosting family at our Robbinsville house. Sometimes the last of our family didn't leave until after ten o'clock at night, after which time Noreen and I and Steven and Kevin would typically drive to our church for the Christmas Eve service. We often would not return home until well past midnight. Steven and Kevin would typically go to bed by 1:00 a.m. and Noreen and I would then take their presents out of their hiding spots and place them under the Christmas tree. It was not unusual for Noreen and me to get to bed between 1:30-2:00.

On Christmas Eve 2001 we went to bed much later. After the candlelight service ended, we drove our church's temporary pastor to the Trenton transit center. He didn't have a car and was trying to catch the last train home to Philadelphia. We were a few minutes late.

"I'll find a cab to take me home," our pastor said when he returned to the minivan where my family waited after dropping him off in the hope that the train would be a few minutes behind schedule. I immediately decided this big-hearted Black clergyman who had just presided over our church's Christmas Eve service deserved better.

"Hop back inside," I said. "We'll be glad to drive you home."

"Really?" he responded, astonished. "You don't have to do that!"

"Of course we will," I replied. For the next hour, the five of us traveled south on highways, over the Delaware River and through the streets of Philadelphia to bring him to his front door. He was very grateful we traveled so far out of our way so late to get him home on Christmas Eve. I was glad to be able to help him out and hoped Steven and Kevin would understand it was simply the right thing to do, particularly in the spirit of Christmas. It was around 2:30 a.m. by the time we returned to our Robbinsville home that night. As usual, Noreen and I waited until Steven and Kevin went to bed to put their gifts under the Christmas tree.

We always told our kids to wake us whenever they got up and wanted to open their presents no matter what time it was, even in 2001. It didn't matter to me whether I got just five or six hours of sleep after a late Christmas Eve. There was no "don't wake us up to open gifts before eight or nine o'clock" rule on Christmas Day in our house. Perhaps this doesn't seem like a big deal to most people. But one Christmas morning after our family moved to the house on Birch Street, my stepfather locked my brother and me in the room where we slept. He didn't unlock the door so we could go to the first floor where our gifts sat under the Christmas tree until he and my mother, whose bedroom was located on the first floor, had woken up and were ready to open gifts. My brother and I were not feeling joyful by this point.

My stepfather nearly killed the Christmas spirit in me. I was determined never to do that with my own children by simply doing the opposite of what my stepfather had done. It was that way with a whole lot of other things as well.

When I was between twelve and fourteen years old, for example, my stepfather liked going to drive-in movies. My mother and Lou rarely wanted to join us, so I would usually be alone in the car with my stepfather. We always saw the movie he wanted to watch. He never asked me what I wanted to see. In contrast, when Noreen and I went to movie theatres with Steven and Kevin while they were growing up, we asked them what movie they wanted to see. And we always enjoyed them.

My wife and I also enjoyed attending concerts with our children. Often times, it was concerts they performed in. Steven worked hard to become an accomplished percussionist from the time he was in middle school through his college years. We attended all of his school performances as well as concerts he performed in with jazz ensembles and elite orchestras. For a few years, we also took in nearly all Steven's gigs with a rock 'n' roll band. We were practically his roadies, helping haul his drum set around in our minivan. Kevin also played in a rock 'n' roll band, and we got a big kick out of watching him perform in front of his teenage classmates.

In contrast to my stepfather, who I would never have dared ask to go to a concert with me when I was a teenager, I brought Steven to shows in Philadelphia, the Garden State Arts Center and Montclair State University in New Jersey that he wanted to attend. (Korn was great!) I must have been the oldest person and Kevin the youngest, at almost twelve, to see the Ben Folds concert at Alexander Hall in Princeton in October of 2002. Noreen and I also enjoyed taking Steven and Kevin to some of the concerts we attended, including Bob Dylan in Camden when they were nearly fourteen and ten years old.

Years later, when Kevin was living in Hoboken, Noreen and I were glad he wanted to join us a few times to see a favorite Cuban American musician of mine, Walter Salas-Humara. I first saw Walter perform at a house concert with his band, the Silos, and instantly became a fan. In his own words, Walter was "conceived in Havana, Cuba and born in New York City." Along with being an accomplished singer, songwriter and guitarist, Walter is a fine painter. My wife and I purchased one of Walter's dog portraits as a wedding gift for a nephew in 2018. I have almost all the music Walter has recorded and, having seen him perform many times, you can accurately conclude I consider him a kindred spirit of sorts.

I never wanted my sons to feel like they owed me expressions of gratitude when I simply did things that any loving, caring parent would naturally be inclined to do, whether it was driving them some place, helping them in some way, or doing something they wanted to do, like going to a game or being at a show. After all, they didn't ask me to be their father. It was a responsibility I willingly took on thanks to God's good graces and a gift and opportunity that I made sure not to squander.

Noreen and I are eternally grateful for the gift of our sons. We've loved Steven and Kevin unconditionally. It's not their jobs on this earth to make us look good and feel great or "earn" things from us. Yes, we're proud of the fine young men they've become. What's most important, though, is that THEY are happy and healthy. I hope the positive legacy Noreen and I leave our sons is that they know how to be good parents to their children should God grace them with such blessings.

I've understood from reading and listening that most children look to emulate how they were raised. I agree with what was written in a 2016 familyrelationshipblog.wordpress.com post, "The Importance of Family:" "Children watch their parents interact with others, make choices and determine right and wrong for themselves, and this impacts how they develop their moral self. Family interactions can build up or break down an individual's self-confidence."

Lou also was a different father than either of his fathers were to him. Like me, he seemed to learn while growing up how NOT to treat his children. Since children often perpetuate the negative parental example they observe growing up, I hope my younger siblings succeed in overcoming the negative example set by their father. My sister Lauren is certainly a different parent—as a single mom, she also finds herself in the father role—than the father and mother she had growing up. And my brother Rob, as challenging as it is for a variety of reasons, gives me the impression he also wants to be a better father.

Being the father of Steven and Kevin is the best thing that ever happened to me. I find it particularly gratifying since I realized by the time

I was thirty it is what I wanted to do more than anything else in life. I posted the following thoughts on my blog, *1400 Characters*, on Father's Day in 2011:

"Being a father has helped me become a much better person. For this, I want to thank my children.

It was only after the birth of my first son 24 years ago that I learned patience. When my second son entered the world four years later, I enhanced my multi-tasking skills so that each of my boys could feel how important they were to me.

Through raising my two sons, I've been reacquainted with appreciating the simple pleasures of life, like waiting for fish to bite a worm on a hook. I've experienced joys and other feelings I nearly forgot about after growing up.

Fatherhood has taught me the nuances of baseball and soccer that can be passed on to young children, and how much fun it can be to get soaking wet running around a field with them. I've learned every rule of soccer, a knowledge that has enabled me to appreciate a match at any level more than ever.

By being a dad, I've learned to appreciate different kinds of music, be it jazz or classical or pop. I've learned how important a drummer is to the sound of a small band or big ensemble. I've even learned what it takes to pack, assemble, and break down a drum set.

Being a father has enabled me to appreciate the value of trying different things, like wrestling or playing lacrosse, acoustic or bass guitar, blackjack, or performing in a school musical. I've also learned that it's fine to move on from one activity to another after giving it an honest try, even after a significant investment in equipment or time.

I've learned to be less selfish by being a father because, when I looked around, I realized I was not the center of my universe. There were children who needed my time, my attention, my energy, and whatever else I could willingly share with them, day after day, in blocks of hours or, at least, minutes.

I've become less materialistic by being a father and seeing my children borrow my clothes and cars. I've learned that I actually own nothing in life. I'm merely in temporary possession of various items, a very liberating feeling, as is the knowledge that money has little value if you don't have loved ones to share it with.

Love? I've felt a fuller, more meaningful sense of love by being a father, be it by changing a diaper, sitting through a late game or performance on a weeknight, providing comfort while watching a doctor stitch a cut, listening, and providing support as a hope is born or vanishes ... or, more often than not, simply by being in the same room with them.

More than anything, I've wanted to help my children in life by being a good father to them. I had no idea, however, that being a father would be so helpful in my own life. For this, I will always remain grateful to my children."

Two friends of mine who are psychologists told me after reading this, "By loving and caring for your sons you not only bestowed upon them the best of fatherhood, you additionally gave the gift of long overdue fatherhood to yourself."

The Father with Kevin and Steven, Noreen, 2004

Chapter 17. The Estranged Stepson: Demise of a Family

In 2006, my mother and stepfather moved to a fifty-five plus community in Jackson, New Jersey. In 2012, weeks before their forty-fifth wedding anniversary, she died of complications from a cardiac procedure.

During her last few years, my mother often found herself short of breath, sometimes from just walking or doing other physically routine things. In 2011, an echocardiogram indicated an issue with her mitral valve caused my mother's shortness of breath. She agreed to have surgery to repair the valve the following winter.

The January day after the surgery was performed, my stepfather was told my mother's aorta tore at the end of the procedure. Her blood pressure was extremely low, and she needed to be monitored closely. When I spoke directly to the surgeon the following morning, he confirmed that although the valve repair was successful, an aortic dissection occurred during the procedure. The surgeon told me it "looked okay" and the "blood flow looked good."

I walked about a mile from my midtown Manhattan office to the hospital where my mother was recuperating from surgery a few times that week to visit her. She did not look well but she smiled and was always happy to see me. I commented when I saw her once that she suddenly bore a striking resemblance to my brother Lou, which made her laugh.

On Friday the 13th, my stepfather reported my mother had a couple of setbacks in the hospital. He specified her heart rhythm was abnormal and fluid was in her lungs. That Sunday morning, my eldest son, Steven, called and told Noreen that while my mother was laughing and talking in her hospital room, she suddenly became unconscious and passed away. Noreen told me the news and I immediately cried louder than

I had ever cried before. Shortly afterward, I was in our minivan while Noreen drove us to the hospital. After we arrived, I learned that my mother's aorta had ripped and leaked blood when doctors attempted to re-start her heart. Her life was over at seventy-five years of age.

The beginning of the end of my relationship with my stepfather began a few years later in 2015, after forty-eight years of trying to please him and realizing our relationship would always continue evolving around his needs and his wants. These included, of course, having his family and others constantly make him look and feel good.

Shortly after my mother passed away, my stepfather was determined to pursue a lawsuit against the hospital where she died. He claimed he wasn't interested in getting money from the hospital but, rather, having the doctor and hospital proven wrong and punished. He was angry at them for the way they handled the surgery and communicated the complications to him afterward. Neither my siblings nor I encouraged him to pursue the lawsuit. He insisted on proceeding with legal action anyway. Shortly afterward, he asked me to be the executor of my mother's estate and co-plaintiff with him in the malpractice suit. Reluctantly, but because I still wanted to placate my stepfather, I agreed. During the next few years, I cooperated with the New York attorney my stepfather retained to move the lawsuit forward. Along with my siblings, I gave a heart-wrenching deposition to the hospital's attorney in 2014.

During this same time, of my stepfather's children, I was the most attentive to his needs. I called and visited him regularly and made sure he continued to feel welcomed and comfortable at my family functions. Even though I knew he and my mother had had an awful marriage, I felt sorry that he lost his spouse. In contrast, I realized that he never seemed to feel sorry that I lost my mother. He asked me and Noreen to remove my mother's clothes and some other possessions from their home while he was away on vacation, which we did despite how emotionally difficult this was for me. As time went on, I saw clearly that he had made my mother's loss all about him and his grieving, even as he started dating other women a year later. He had no support to give to me or my siblings about the loss of our mother.

By 2015, my stepfather seemed to start losing his interest in the lawsuit. He had begun a relationship with a woman who had also lost her spouse recently and the two of them started regularly posting "mushy" and other romantic pictures and words on *Facebook*. These postings made it appear he was happy and had moved on. I asked my stepfather not to do this while we were involved in a lawsuit with the hospital. The attorney he retained told him to "get off Facebook altogether." My stepfather ignored us for a few more months until I implored him to stop the posts. I instructed him over the phone how to de-activate his *Facebook* account. Instead of being apologetic about being selfish, lacking empathy for his deceased wife's children and inconveniencing me, he accused me of bullying him and grudgingly de-activated his account while we were on the phone. But his girlfriend continued with some posts of the two of them. It was clear that he hadn't asked her to stop posting as well.

In 2017, my stepfather indicated to his attorney and me he wanted to reach a settlement with the hospital. It was obvious the lawsuit he had decided to pursue against the advice of many people was now a nuisance to him. I told my stepfather that a settlement would likely involve no admission of wrongdoing by the hospital. I reminded him of why he had initiated this legal action in the first place. If getting money from the hospital was not the goal of the lawsuit, I told my stepfather and the attorney we should remain open to a trial. The attorney strongly advocated for a settlement, citing the preparation and risky outcome of a trial.

I met with my stepfather at the clubhouse of his fifty-five plus community to talk one-on-one about the lawsuit, how he intended to divide the settlement money (he refused to answer this question) and, more generally, our deteriorating relationship. He got up and walked out of the room when he did not like what I was saying, which included how difficult it was to be his stepson. In hindsight, his refusal to listen and reason was typical of how he handled difficult conversations with me and other family members.

If I were my stepfather, I would have thought long and hard about how to proceed with the lawsuit in order to accomplish his objectives. I would perhaps have done some soul searching about what his stepson had said about their relationship during the meeting. Instead, a few weeks later, I received a letter from a New Jersey attorney my stepfather had retained. The letter threatened to seek my "removal as executor for breach of fiduciary duty." I sought counsel on how to respond to this threat and resolve the lawsuit situation. I spoke with Uncle John, a New York lawyer, and wound up following the advice of my own attorney, who after I truthfully went over all that had transpired questioned why I would ever want to speak to my stepfather again. After negotiating with my stepfather through his attorney how the settlement funds should be divided—my stepfather made sure he pocketed more than twice the amount his four children combined received despite previously claiming he didn't care about the money—I agreed to enter into a settlement with the hospital.

By the time the lawsuit with the hospital was settled, our family was deeply divided. As explained before, Lauren had already broken off her relationship with her father a few years earlier. The manner in which he behaved as the lawsuit unfolded confirmed her conclusion he was a narcissist with mental issues who would never change for the better. By this point, I no longer wanted to see or talk to my stepfather ever again. I agreed with my sister that he was a toxic person who would never

change. Lou never had a good relationship or desire to pay much attention to our stepfather, although after all this time away he still speaks
with him a few times a year out of pity. Only my brother Rob and his
wife, who my stepfather had despised just a few years earlier, seemed on
good terms with him by the time the lawsuit was settled.

Despite the deep division within our family, my stepfather sent out an
email after the lawsuit was settled saying, "I am glad that I didn't take
the advice of some which was to drop the lawsuit for my peace of mind.
And I feel that it accomplished my original purpose—to let the hospital know that the way they dealt with the family involved (us) was unac-
ceptable." Some of his children and grown grandchildren were offend-
ed by my stepfather's message, knowing how he had gained financially without the doctor or hospital being on record for any wrongdoing.
Meanwhile, relations within our extended family had broken down or
deteriorated to a pile of rubble.

I have tried to figure out why my stepfather behaves the way he does.
For example, does he know when he lies, or does he have a mental illness? I've wanted to know why he has a constant, unsatiable need to be
thanked and thanked again for everything he does that might possibly
be helpful to someone. I've wanted to understand why he always wants
to be the center of attention, why everything anyone does or says needs
to be pleasing to him or else it is unimportant or, worse yet, offensive. I
believe that my sister is correct in concluding her father has narcissistic
personality disorder and other mental issues. I have not observed this
disorder in his siblings, nor do I believe his parents behaved as if they
were narcissistic or had a mental illness. How did my stepfather get this
way?

I will probably never know the answer. My stepfather told me several
times, though, how his life changed when his father returned home after World War II. My stepfather was born a few months after his fa-

ther was sent overseas and he was past his second birthday when his father first saw him. Apparently, he was a spoiled child by then, coddled by grandparents and other family members. When his father returned home, he insisted everyone stop calling his son by his nickname and tried to insert himself as the main authority figure in his child's life. This must have been traumatic for my young stepfather, who in the following two years found himself sharing his parents' attention with a younger brother and sister.

My stepfather never spoke well of his father, who never acted fully satisfied with his eldest son. His father could be harsh and judgmental, for sure, but he generally seemed to speak more kindly of his second son, who served in Vietnam, and of his daughter. But my stepfather also never spoke well of his mother. For that matter, I don't remember him having a kind word to say about his brother or sister. Actually, my stepfather never spoke well of anyone to me when there was no one else around: He was particularly harsh toward those who I spoke well of or admired.

When I spoke positively about his parents, who always treated me like a good step grandson and embraced my wife and children like true family, he found something negative to say about them. When I said that his brother looked good after losing weight, he quickly responded, "I think he looks awful." Similarly, when he heard someone speak positively about his sister, he typically responded with a negative comment. He also spoke poorly about those he considered friends and never had anything but critical observations to share about my in-laws from the time I got married. Speaking to my sister in recent years, I learned that he spoke negatively about me to her whenever she said something positive about me to him.

When my stepfather noticed how much I liked an athlete like Joe Namath or an entertainer like Bob Dylan or politician like Ronald Reagan, he quickly shot them down. I could go on and on with examples, as could my sister. Two psychologist friends of mine believe my stepfather's negative words about others can be traced back to his father's negative attitude about his eldest son.

It was not until many years later that I came to the conclusion that my stepfather probably never had anything good to say about anybody—unless they kissed his ass or did something extraordinary to make him look or feel great—because he wanted to hoard all good words and adulation for himself. He wanted anything good that was said to be all about him; he didn't want competition for praise from other people! I did not observe this kind of behavior in his father.

My relationship with a stepfather whose surname I took on and appeased for forty-eight years by making him look and feel good is nonexistent now.

Mom and the Cuban American, 1999

Chapter 18. El Sobrino: Reconnecting Family Roots

On Thanksgiving Day 2007, my wife, our sons, and I sat down for a traditional turkey dinner with some favorite Cuban side dishes with Tía Gloria, Tío Basi and Cousin Anna in Hialeah, Florida. It was the first time in memory I celebrated a holiday with the Lopez side of my family, and it marked the start of a solid reconnection with them. I will always remember how ecstatic Gloria was to be with me, her *sobrino* (nephew), and my family that day.

My fondest memory of my paternal side of the family before that Thanksgiving was when they arrived to live in Brooklyn, New York after immigrating from Cuba in the autumn of 1966. Tía Gloria, Cousin Anna, Abuela Nina and Abuelo Elpidio had left their home on the island with little more than the clothes on their back. Anna, who is six months younger than me, was so excited to be able to drink as much milk as she wanted when her family arrived at the Miami Freedom Tower, the immigration processing center for Cubans, just before she turned ten. Soon after Fidel Castro took power in Cuba, dairy products were rationed until a child turned seven years old. After that, the ration was taken away, making it virtually impossible for children older than seven to have any milk. Anna drank a lot of milk during her first few days in the U.S., and to this day enjoys consuming whole milk from red and white cartons that remind her of the dairy products she had as a new immigrant.

Tía Gloria did not have the revolutionary spirit after Fidel Castro took power in Cuba. She refused to dress in the combat fatigues she was encouraged to wear to show her support for his government at her office. After Gloria arrived in New York, she and Cousin Anna and my grandparents stayed a month in Tío Pete's apartment with his wife and son.

She found a job within a week and moved into an apartment in Brooklyn with her daughter and parents. While waiting for Uncle Basi, who she married by proxy, to arrive, she took on a second and third job to support her daughter and parents. Abuela Nina cleaned the homes of affluent people in Brooklyn Heights to supplement her daughter's income and helped furnish their apartment with hand-me-downs from her clients. Abuelo Elpidio, who had a heart condition, helped by walking his granddaughter, Anna, to school and taking care of shopping and cooking for the family. Gloria worked until she was over eighty years old (or young, since she always looked and acted younger than her age), taking pride that she did not need any government handouts in her adopted country. As she got older, she was quick to point out that she was more American than Cuban since she had lived the majority of her life in the U.S.

Tía Gloria's story is not unusual for Cubans who left the island during the first fifteen years of the Revolution. According to a Pew Research Center report, *Hispanic Trends*, published in 2006, "Compared with the rest of the Hispanic population in the United States, Cubans are older, have a higher level of education, higher median household income and higher rate of home ownership ... The initial exodus primarily consisted of upper and upper middle-class families in professional and managerial occupations. The second wave, from about 1965 to 1974, featured orderly departure programs administered by the U.S and Cuban governments. The so-called 'freedom flights' brought middle- and working-class Cubans to the United States."

In November of 1966, shortly after arriving in New York from Cuba via Florida, my paternal family, including my father, Humberto, got together at Tío Pete's Brooklyn apartment to celebrate Cousin Anna's tenth birthday. Lou and I were there with my mother, who was just a couple of months away from marrying my stepfather. To my mother and Tía Gloria's credit, they stayed in touch after our family moved to

New Jersey and progressed with our new lives. My mother was never estranged from my father's family and their best friends. This helped me remain connected with them as I grew up.

Another memory I have of my paternal family from around that time is Abuelo Elpidio's funeral. He passed away from a heart attack at home with Abuela Nina, Tía Gloria and Cousin Anna beside him in October of 1968. It was just a couple of weeks after Gloria's second husband, Tío Basi, was reunited with the family after leaving Cuba via Spain. I remember Elpidio as a kind, gentle, soft-spoken man. I can still distinctly recall the sound of his voice, which he sometimes used to reprimand his eldest son (my father) for not properly supporting his two children. His funeral was extremely sad, not just because he died before reaching the age of sixty, but because his wife, Nina, insisted on having a Jehovah's Witness preacher at the funeral home. Nina had converted, but Elpidio and other family members remained Catholic. My father and others walked out of the room when the Jehovah's Witness preacher started talking, and Tío Pete was very angry and hot-tempered that night.

I never felt a close connection to Abuela Nina. She seemed hurt and sad on the few occasions I saw her during the last twenty years of her life. It made Lou and me feel guilty we had strayed from her family, almost as if it was our fault that her son, my father, was divorced from our mother and we had started new lives with a stepfather and his last name. Many years later I learned that my father was Nina's favorite son. Humberto may have been a good son to my grandparents, a good brother to Tía Gloria and Tío Pete and a good uncle to Cousin Anna. But Nina was blind to her son's failures as a husband to Elena and father to Lou and me.

I did not quite get that same feeling from Tía Gloria, who was also disappointed that her *sobrinos*, Lou and I, were not actively part of her

life. But she seemed understanding of the situation and happy to enjoy our company when we were together. Gloria and Tío Basi were at
my wedding in 1981, as were some close family friends from Brooklyn.
Noreen and I also saw them on a few other occasions after we got married, sometimes in Brooklyn and later in Florida after they moved.

I visited Tía Gloria, Tío Basi and Cousin Anna and their families in the
summer of 1987 when Noreen and I and our infant son, Steven, were
staying in Florida for a few weeks because of my work. It was great to
be with them and their children. Astonishingly, Gloria and her daughter Anna, born twenty years apart, had both been pregnant at the same
time about ten years earlier and had children just a few weeks apart in
age. Abuela Nina sat quietly by herself during our visit—Alzheimer's
had begun affecting her by this point. It was the last time I remember
seeing her.

I barely kept in touch with Tía Gloria, Tío Basi and Cousin Anna for
several years afterward, but my mother continued regularly communi-
cating with her ex-sister-in-law and kept everyone informed about each
other's families. When Noreen and I planned to vacation in Florida
with Steven and Kevin in 2007, Gloria insisted we have Thanksgiving
dinner with her, Basi and Anna in Hialeah rather than at the Versailles
Restaurant in Miami as we had originally planned. I'm glad we did! It
was wonderful for all of us to reconnect and I was especially glad Steven
and Kevin, ages twenty-one and seventeen, respectively, by this point,
got to experience the holiday with a Cuban part of the family previously unfamiliar to them.

After that Thanksgiving Day of 2007, I made it a point to call Tía Gloria on the phone on that holiday for several years. I visited her home
again in the spring of 2011, while I was in Miami on business. The
following year, it was my voice she heard when the phone rang and
she learned that her ex-sister-in-law, my mother who she referred to as

Elenita, had passed away. I am very grateful the two of them stayed close for dozens of years after my parents divorced.

In 2015, I returned to Florida with Lou and his wife, who had never visited Tía Gloria and Tío Basi's Hialeah home. Gloria was ecstatic to reconnect with her long-lost nephew, who she had not seen since my wedding day thirty-four years earlier. During that trip, Cousin Anna took Lou and his wife and me to Calle Ocho, the main street in the Little Havana neighborhood of Miami. It was my first time there and I was excited to be walking around the strongest Cuban environment outside of the island nation itself. Our experience was capped off with a stop at the Versailles Restaurant, "The World's Most Famous Cuban Restaurant^{SM}." I stood by the café window wearing my guayabera shirt, popular with many Cuban men, and sipped a heavenly *café con leche*.

Noreen and I have returned to visit Tía Gloria, Tío Basi and Cousin Anna in Florida a couple of times since then, including during the winter of 2020 with Lou and his wife.

Better late than never, it has been gratifying for everyone on my paternal side of the family to be reconnected. Blood can indeed be good when it is thick and sweet like Cuban coffee.

El Sobrino, Tia Gloria, Cousin Anna, Tio Basi, 2007

Chapter 19. El Español: Visiting the Motherland

In the spring of 2019, as Noreen and I prepared to visit *España* (Spain) for the first time, I reached out to Cousin Anna in Florida about our ancestors who I knew were exclusively *Español* (Spanish) before migrating to Cuba. Indeed, she confirmed, all our ancestors were from Spain or the Canary Islands. Documents she had indicated that some of our family hailed from the Andalusia region in the south and Madrid, and most likely migrated to Cuba between 1770-1810. On my mother's side, I had been told years ago that all of my ancestors were from Spain and the Canary Islands with the possible exception of a branch of Abuela Belen's family, which may have originated in Portugal. All of my mother's side of the family migrated to Cuba by around 1870. In addition to being the land of my father and mother and four grandparents, Cuba is therefore the birthplace of all eight of my great grandparents as well as at least half of my great-great-grandparents.

According to an article by Maria Carmen Faus Pujol of the University of Zaragoza posted in cubaheritage.org, "The European heritage of Cubans comes primarily from one source: the Spaniards (including Canarians, Asturians, Catalans, Galicians and Castilians). The native white population are nearly all descendants of the Spaniards and most non-white Cubans also have Spanish ancestry."

My pre-Cuban Spanish ancestry confirmed, I spent eight enlightening and entertaining days in Madrid, Toledo, Cordoba, Sevilla, Granada, Valencia, Montserrat, and Barcelona with Noreen. We were surrounded by wonderful people (many who shared my physical characteristics), fascinating sights and plenty of great coffee and food. When I returned home, I shared the following thoughts on my blog:

"I walked past them on the streets of Madrid, Barcelona and other cities in Spain. Many of them had my complexion, my eyes, my hair. Several of the faces bore the look my wife had become familiar with over the years. For sure, I was among my people. At the very least, I was among people whose distant ancestry I shared. No doubt, there were lots of them who had the same Lopez, Suarez, Castro and possibly Valdés surnames as my parents, grandparents, and those in the previous generations of our family who migrated from Spain to Cuba 150-250 years ago. I never felt so comfortable, so at home, in a foreign land."

It is no surprise that my ancestry composition, according to a 23andMe DNA test, is 86 percent Spanish and Portuguese and, overall, 90 percent Southern European. The 23andMe DNA test found the strongest evidence of my ancestry in the Canary Islands of Spain, followed by the Andalusia, Galicia, Asturias, Castile and Leon, Cantabria, and Madrid areas. There was also strong evidence of ancestry from the Azores and Madeira islands of Portugal. No wonder my ancestors emigrated to another island, Cuba. And little wonder my parents many years later left Cuba for another island, Manhattan!

I hope to return to Cuba with Lou when the time is right. We will visit the Jaimanitas neighborhood of Havana where we spent time during our pre-school years. I also look forward to going back to Spain to see the finished Basilica de la Sagrada Familia in Barcelona with millions of Spaniards and people of Spanish ancestry. I hope to learn about other parts of our motherland's history and culture.

El Español in Spain, 2019

Postscript: Fatherlands: Identities of a Cuban American

One morning during the middle of April in 2020, a sixty-three-year-old man stood on the balcony of the Long Branch beachfront condominium unit he shared with his wife. He saw a group of surfers in the ocean, waiting to jump on their boards to ride a wave. A coronavirus pandemic was sweeping across New Jersey, the U.S., and much of the world on this day, but the man remained focused on all the blessings life had bestowed on him. He thought about all the waves he had rode during his twisting and turning journey through life and those that remained to be navigated in the years ahead. That man was me.

El niño. The second son. The young boy. The nephew. The happy camper. The outcast. The younger sibling. The big brother. The proud brother. The sportswriter. The card shark. The Lopez and Bruns. The pirate. The young star and old guy. The husband. The father. The estranged stepson. El sobrino. El Español. These have been parts of my identity during my journey through life. Perhaps you were known by some of these or similar labels during your own life. I believe everyone, whether or not they are a child of immigrants or grew up in a non-traditional household, has an identity made up of parts they have been known by, unwittingly or otherwise, during their journey through life.

Decades after my parents divorced in New York City and my struggle starting a new life in New Jersey, I continue reaching deep inside of me and taking stock of who I am and what I'm not. Like that boy who grew up in New York after living in Cuba and then moved to New Jersey, I have retained a sense of my identity while realizing and accepting I'm different than many of the people around me. Isn't each one of us different in some way or another? And, ironically, isn't that what makes all of us alike?

The nearly non-existent relationship I had with my biological father taught me to be a caring and responsible person. The difficult experiences with my stepfather led me to value truthfulness and empathy more than ever. These values and some others I learned from observing my family helped to establish the foundation for my marriage and subsequent ability to raise my children with love and kindness. Values I learned as a first-generation Cuban American of Spanish descent have also helped me grow my career and sustain a good quality of life for my family.

My journey is not done. Neither is yours. We will always be works in progress. Although I have a stronger sense of my identity, I continue learning from my past experiences and current challenges. I remain interested in knowing more about other people around our diverse world whose identities are being transformed by immigration, separation, condemnation, assimilation, cultural changes or, ultimately, realization of just who they are and what they are not. I will continue focusing on the positive and promising in my life and being well prepared for the remaining journey of my identity. I encourage you to do the same!

Poem: Family Family

Swish, swish, "What goes on out there?"

Some yelling, some tears, much heartache.

"Ah, a boy! How cute. He looks just like me."

More yelling, more tears, lots of heartache.

Disappointment. Embarrassment. Shame.

The boy goes out to sail.

The winds blow east, they blow west.

The clouds thicken, then pour rain.

He can barely stand.

The forces knock him down

and he falls in the water.

Drenched, he climbs back onboard

naked, shivering, crying.

Over and over.

Disappointment. Embarrassment. Shame.

Family.

The boy grows into a man.

He can withstand the wind.

The rain bounces off his skin.

He jumps into the water

and climbs back onto the boat.

He dries himself off slowly

and looks up at the sun,

eyes closed, heart open.

Swish, swish, "What goes on out there?"

Some lullabies, some smiles, some joy.

"Ah, a boy! How cute! He looks just like me."

More lullabies, more smiles, lots of joy.

Satisfaction. Confidence. Pride.

The man goes out to sail.

He steers his boat calmly, deftly.

Protected from a passing shower,

he resumes enjoying his time at sea.

The sunset is beautiful

and he admires the view of it.

Back ashore, he looks forward

to a restful, fulfilling evening.

Over and over.

Satisfaction. Confidence. Pride.

Family.

(Postscript:)

Mix some light tones into a dark color

and a medium shade appears.

Add brighter tones into a medium color

and a lighter hue appears.

Just like the family some people

are born into.

Just like the family some people

create for their loved ones.

From *1400 Characters* blog; first published July 4, 2018, and read that day at the 4th Pier Village Poetry Festival in Long Branch

The Poet, 2018

Appendix: Cuban Immigration in the United States

According to the *U.S. Department of Justice Statistical Yearbook* of the Immigration and Naturalization Service published in 1996, just 26,313 Cubans migrated to the U.S. in the years between 1941-50, when my maternal grandmother, Abuela Belen, arrived in New York City. That is just a third of the number that migrated in the following decade (many in 1959 alone, I'm certain), when my mother and father arrived in New York City, and a very small fraction of the numbers that came to the country from the island in later decades.

Between 1961-70, for example, 208,536 Cubans migrated to the U.S., many via the Freedom Flights between Varadero, Cuba, and Miami. This is how my paternal grandparents, Abuelo Elpidio and Abuela Nina, aunt (Tía Gloria) and Cousin Anna arrived in 1966.

The number of Cuban immigrants between 1971-80 was even higher, 264,863, nearly half of whom arrived in a variety of watercrafts during the exodus from the port of Mariel, Cuba, in the spring and summer of 1980. Cubans who arrived in 1980 have typically been referred to as "Marielitos." Contrary to what some people believe, only a small fraction of Marielitos were what the U.S. government considered criminals.

Between 1981-90, the number of Cuban immigrants declined to 144,578. That number declined further to approximately 100,000 between 1990-2000, according to the U.S. Census Bureau, even with a spike in the early 1990s when Cuba entered a "special period" of economic hardship after the collapse of the Soviet Union. A significant number of Cuban refugees utilized makeshift rafts to flee the island in 1994 and were referred to as "balseros" (rafters). That same year, the two countries reached an agreement allowing 20,000 Cubans to legally leave for the United States each year. In 1995, the U.S. began implementing its "wet feet, dry feet" policy of not admitting Cubans intercepted in U.S. waters but allowing those who made it ashore to remain.

During the first ten years of the new millennium, the number of Cuban immigrants rose again to approximately 232,000, which was above the number legally permitted to leave directly to the U.S. The number continued rising between 2011-2018, when approximately 239,000 Cubans entered the U.S. According to the Pew Research Center, 55,000 immigrated during 2016 alone. That same year, the U.S. Coast Guard apprehended 5,263 Cubans at sea. All were returned to Cuba or a third country.

Acknowledgments

First and foremost, I want to thank my wife and all the family members who encouraged me as I worked on this book. You know who you are and how grateful I am for your support as I developed what I often described as "the book I was meant to write." I am particularly thankful for the thoughtful feedback you provided on the first draft and the additional information and ideas you shared to make this a better book.

I am also grateful to Diane and Marshall Harth for challenging me to dig deeper into parts of my life and my feelings in order to make this a better book. In addition, I want to thank the former Saint Paul the Apostle School and Carteret School classmates who were kind enough to share their distant memories of me.

A special thank you goes to Patricia Perry Donovan, the wife of a former corporate communication colleague of mine who carved out time from her busy schedule to edit my second draft and share many suggestions for making this book better. Patricia is an award-winning short story writer and author of two outstanding novels, *At Wave's End* (2017) and *Deliver Her* (2016) published by Lake Union.

I also want to thank Hank Gola, a former *Herald-News* colleague who went on to a distinguished sports writing career and is the author of one of the best non-fiction works I've ever read, *City of Champions* (2018) published by Tatra Press, which was clearly a labor of love and the book he was meant to write. Hank challenged me to make my book more descriptive and, along with Patricia, provided valuable advice on how best to get it in the hands of readers like you.

I also want to acknowledge the outstanding editing of my manuscript by Diane Stockwell, a fellow New Yorker whose experience with other Cuban American writers helped alleviate some of my concerns as a first-time author. I also want to thank Jim Redzinak, a graphic artist I first met almost 40 years ago, for designing the cover of my memoir. I hope Diane and Jim's efforts help this book stand out from most others.

This book had its origins in an August of 2014 blog post about my mother moving from New York City to Bloomfield, New Jersey during the late 1960s. I expanded on it after Laurie Roemmele, a daughter of the former *Bloomfield Life* and *Independent Press* editor, read a *Facebook* post in January of 2016 about my name change and asked me to contribute a chapter for a book project about the personal struggles some individuals have overcome. When I shared what I drafted with some family and friends, I was encouraged to expand the ten-page chapter to a full-length book. It was a slow process at first since I was quite busy as a self-employed communication consultant. But when the coronavirus pandemic struck the U.S. in March of 2020 and curtailed many day-to-day activities, I took advantage of the opportunity to spend more time on the book. I want to thank Laurie for helping get me started on what eventually became this book, but I will never thank the pandemic for helping me to finish it so quickly!

September 14, 2021

About the author

Charles Lopez was born to Cuban immigrants who settled in New York City before the Revolution. After his parents divorced and he returned from an extended stay in Cuba, he began learning to speak English. Five years later his mother remarried, he moved to New Jersey and became known as Charles Bruns. He began working as a journalist while a teenager and launched his corporate communication career during college. Along the way, he married and raised a family. But he never stopped thinking about who he is and what he isn't or writing in his second language. *Fatherlands: Identities of a Cuban American* is his debut book.

The Author, 2021

Made in United States
North Haven, CT
12 October 2021